MW01492702

Gigi Romano

The Derby of the Eternal Enemies: Olympiacos vs. Panathinaikos - A Rivalry that Defines Greek Football

Copyright © 2025 by Gigi Romano

All rights reserved.

First Edition published in April 2025

No part of this book may be copied, stored, or shared in any form—whether by photocopy, recording, or digital transmission—without the express written consent of the publisher. Exceptions are made for brief quotations used in reviews, scholarly articles, or other non-commercial writings, as allowed under applicable copyright law.

This work, in all its forms, is protected by intellectual property law. Unauthorized use, reproduction, or distribution is a violation and may be subject to legal action.

Thank you for respecting the rights of the author and publisher.

The Derby of the Eternal Enemies: Olympiacos vs. Panathinaikos - A Rivalry that Defines Greek Football

Table of Contents

Chapter 13: *The Fans Beyond the Stadium*

Chapter 14: *The Future of the Derby*

Conclusion

The enduring significance of the Derby of the Eternal Enemies in Greek football and culture

Appendices

Appendix A: *Statistics of Key Matches and Results*

Appendix B: *Notable Players in the Rivalry's History*

Appendix C: *A Timeline of Key Moments in the Derby*

Appendix D: *Fan Culture and the Role of Ultras*

Appendix E: *Notable Managers and Their Impact on the Rivalry*

Introduction: The Rivalry That Defines Greek Football – A History of the Derby

In the heart of Athens, amidst the bustling streets, the coffee shops, and the clamor of daily life, there exists a rivalry that transcends sport. The Derby of the Eternal Enemies, a name given to the fierce clashes between Olympiacos and Panathinaikos, is more than just a football match. It is a symbol of the soul of Greek football, a battleground where passion, history, and identity collide.

For nearly a century, these two clubs have represented more than just their respective fanbases. They are the personification of two ideologies, two philosophies, and two histories. Olympiacos, with its roots firmly planted in the working-class districts of Piraeus, carries with it a sense of pride tied to the port city and its industrial might. Panathinaikos, born in the wealthier districts of central Athens, represents the elite, the old-world traditions of the Greek capital, a symbol of intellectual and cultural sophistication. This stark contrast, both in geography and class, has contributed to a rivalry unlike any other in the world.

The first encounter between Olympiacos and Panathinaikos came in 1925, but it was not until much later that the true intensity of their rivalry began to take shape. Over the years, the fixture has evolved into a symbolic battle for supremacy, not only on the football pitch but in every aspect of Greek life. From the boardrooms of both clubs to the terraces where passionate fans wave their flags, the stakes of this derby are immeasurable.

Throughout the decades, this rivalry has produced unforgettable moments—players whose names are etched in Greek footballing folklore, managers whose decisions could make or break the very fabric of their teams, and matches that have kept millions of spectators on the edge of their seats. The fierce competition between the two clubs is more than just a clash of football teams; it's a reflection of Greek society itself— its divisions, its pride, and its undying passion for the beautiful game.

For Olympiacos and Panathinaikos, every derby is not just a match, but a declaration of who they are and what they stand for. It's a contest to claim the title of Athens' greatest football club, to define a legacy that will last for generations to come.

This book takes you on a journey through the history of this legendary rivalry. From the very first encounter between Olympiacos and Panathinaikos to the modern-day derbies that continue to electrify Greek football fans, we will explore the key moments, the unforgettable players, the iconic matches, and the culture that has made this rivalry one of the fiercest and most passionate in the world.

The Derby of the Eternal Enemies is a spectacle that demands attention, respect, and admiration. It is the beating heart of Greek football, and its story is one that must be told.

Chapter 1: The Birth of the Rivalry

Origins of Olympiacos and Panathinaikos

The story of the Derby of the Eternal Enemies begins with the origins of two of Greece's most famous football clubs: Olympiacos and Panathinaikos. Their rivalry did not arise overnight, but instead grew from a deep-seated connection to Athens' rich history, contrasting social classes, and competing visions of Greek identity.

Olympiacos was founded in 1925, in Piraeus, the bustling port city of Athens. A club born from the working-class communities, it immediately represented the pulse of the industrial and labor-heavy side of Athens. The club's establishment in Piraeus, an area linked to the everyday struggles and the grit of the people, meant it was a natural extension of the working-class movement. Olympiacos, with its red and white colors, soon became a symbol for the common man, a place where the working classes could channel their energy, hopes, and passion for sport.

In contrast, Panathinaikos was established earlier, in 1908, in the heart of Athens, representing a different class altogether. The club's creation came during a period of national consolidation and a rapidly changing Greece. Panathinaikos, named after the famous

Panathenaic Games, symbolized the cultural and intellectual side of Athens. Its green and white colors, chosen to represent Athens' glory, were a nod to the ancient traditions of the Greek capital. The club was associated with the elite and the bourgeoisie, attracting a following from Athens' upper class, academics, and intellectuals.

The contrasting origins of these two clubs, rooted in different socioeconomic classes, became the foundation of the fierce rivalry that would follow. Olympiacos, born out of Piraeus' industrial heartland, became synonymous with the working-class, while Panathinaikos, a club representing the more cosmopolitan and aristocratic Athenian society, was a symbol of the elite. These origins created a divide that went far beyond the football pitch, influencing the way each club was perceived by their supporters and their role in Greek society.

Early Encounters Between the Two Clubs

The first encounter between Olympiacos and Panathinaikos came in the early years of the clubs' existence. While the two teams initially competed in local tournaments and friendlies, their clashes were often symbolic of the larger social and political divides in Greece.

Their first significant meeting took place in 1925. Though the match was not as internationally recognized as the derbies would later become, it was a momentous occasion for both clubs. The fixture was a chance for both sides to prove their dominance on the field and to claim the title of Athens' greatest team. However, this was just the beginning of what would soon become one of the most heated rivalries in football history.

As the years passed and both clubs found success in the Greek football scene, the fixtures between Olympiacos and Panathinaikos grew more intense. Each match was a battle not only for points but for pride. Olympiacos, with its fiery determination, became known for its aggressive playing style, while Panathinaikos' technical precision was admired and respected. The matches between the two clubs started to take on a ritualistic importance, with both fanbases eagerly anticipating the moments when their teams would face off.

The Cultural and Social Divisions That Fueled the Rivalry

The fierce rivalry between Olympiacos and Panathinaikos was not simply the result of competition on the pitch; it was a reflection of Greece's deep cultural and social divisions. These divisions were influenced by class, politics, and history, which added layers of complexity to the matches.

At its core, the rivalry mirrored the social structure of Athens itself. Piraeus, where Olympiacos was based, had a large working-class population that was often in direct contrast to the wealthier and more intellectual elite in central Athens, where Panathinaikos called home. This divide was not just geographic but also reflected the deeper political and cultural struggles that were taking place in Greece during the early 20th century.

In a time when Greece was still finding its identity as a modern nation, the rivalry between Olympiacos and Panathinaikos became symbolic of these tensions. Olympiacos, representing the working class, often found itself at odds with the aristocratic and intellectual nature of Panathinaikos, which stood as a bastion of the traditional elite. The passion of the supporters, each side fervently defending their team, was tied to their own sense of identity and pride in their social class.

The clubs also represented different political ideologies. Olympiacos' roots in Piraeus aligned with the more left-wing, socialist sentiments of the working class, while Panathinaikos, with its more affluent fanbase, attracted those who were aligned with the right-wing establishment. The political undertones of the rivalry became pronounced during times of political unrest, with the matches taking on added significance as a platform for expressing broader societal frustrations.

In this context, the derby was about more than just football. It became a battleground for the working class and the elite, for the left and the right, and for two distinct visions of Greek society. The matches were often more than just about winning; they were a way for the supporters to affirm their place in society, to challenge the dominance of the other, and to assert their pride.

As Olympiacos and Panathinaikos continued to grow and evolve, so too did their rivalry. It would come to symbolize not just the battle for supremacy on the field, but also the wider struggle for identity, power, and recognition in Greek society.

Chapter 2: The Rise of Olympiacos and Panathinaikos

The Growth of Both Clubs Through the 20th Century

As Greece moved through the tumultuous 20th century, Olympiacos and Panathinaikos grew to become the dominant forces in Greek football, with each club cultivating its own legacy, driven by ambition, fierce rivalries, and the ever-present desire to be the best.

For Olympiacos, the growth began with a deep connection to Piraeus and its working-class roots. The club's initial success was built on determination and grit, with its early years marked by local competitions, where Olympiacos first established its identity. By the 1930s, Olympiacos was firmly cementing its reputation as a footballing powerhouse, clinching national championships and dominating the domestic scene. Its first major success came in 1934 when it won the Greek Championship, a victory that marked the beginning of a long period of dominance. The club's passion for success and drive to be the best was evident in every match, and by the post-war years, Olympiacos was an undeniable force in Greek football.

Panathinaikos, on the other hand, had always carried an air of prestige, dating back to its establishment in 1908.

As Athens' elite team, it swiftly rose to prominence during the early 20th century, consistently competing for national titles. By the 1930s, Panathinaikos had already won its first Greek Championship, solidifying its place among Greece's footballing elite. The club's emphasis on technical skill and finesse made it a favorite of the more intellectual and affluent sectors of Athenian society. Unlike Olympiacos, whose early strength was based on hard work and unity, Panathinaikos capitalized on a more methodical, disciplined approach to the game, often showcasing a superior technical style that was admired by fans across the country.

By the mid-20th century, both clubs had experienced sustained success. Olympiacos, consistently on top of the domestic league, built a winning tradition that became synonymous with their identity. Panathinaikos, in turn, maintained its status as a club that represented Athens' finest, with a roster of players who were not only skilled but also embodying the values of the club.

Key Players and Moments in the Early Years

Throughout the 20th century, certain players and moments defined the course of both clubs, shaping the narrative of Greek football and their rivalry. For Olympiacos, players like Kostas Nestoridis, one of the most prolific and revered forwards in the club's history, became icons. His skill on the ball, sharp finishing, and leadership on the pitch made him a key figure during Olympiacos' rise to national prominence in the 1950s and 1960s.

Panathinaikos, on the other hand, produced its own set of legends. One such player was Giannis Patikas, who led Panathinaikos in the 1950s and became known for his creativity and vision. Another was the legendary Mimis Domazos, who helped elevate the club's stature in the 1960s and 1970s, making numerous contributions to the team's domestic and international successes. These players, along with others, contributed significantly to their clubs' sustained success and laid the foundations for the fierce clashes that would come to define the derby.

Perhaps the most defining moment in the early years for Panathinaikos came in 1971 when the club reached the European Cup final, marking a historic achievement in Greek football. Although they lost to Ajax, Panathinaikos' journey to the final cemented their reputation as one of the top footballing forces in Europe. It was a moment of pride for their fans, who felt the club was on the verge of a new chapter in its storied history.

For Olympiacos, the 1960s and 1970s saw the club win numerous league titles, solidifying their status as

Greece's most successful club at the time. Their competitive nature on the field, combined with their unyielding hunger for success, created an atmosphere of fierce loyalty among their supporters. Each trophy win further entrenched Olympiacos as a symbol of pride for the working class of Piraeus.

The Development of Fan Culture and Ultras

As Olympiacos and Panathinaikos began to dominate the Greek football scene, a new element emerged that would play a crucial role in the rivalry—the fans. The passionate supporters of both clubs created cultures that were both unique and integral to the identity of each team.

The fan culture surrounding Olympiacos began to take shape in the 1960s and 1970s. The club's supporters were known for their fervent devotion and unwavering loyalty. This loyalty became manifest in the creation of the first organized fan groups, which began to travel with the team to away matches, creating an atmosphere of unity and collective passion. The fan base quickly became known for their intense energy, often producing a sea of red and white in the stands, creating an intimidating and electrifying presence. The Olympiacos supporters, led by the infamous "Gate 7" group, were among the most vocal and aggressive in

Greek football, with their chants, flags, and relentless support forming a unique part of the team's identity.

For Panathinaikos, fan culture developed in parallel but with a different flavor. The supporters of Panathinaikos, while equally passionate, maintained a more traditional approach to their fan groups, focusing on creating an elegant and organized atmosphere in the stands. The club's more affluent fanbase fostered a different type of supporters' culture, one that was based on tradition, history, and the pride of representing Athens' elite. Nevertheless, by the 1980s, Panathinaikos fans, particularly the "Gate 13" ultras, began to make their presence felt in a more organized and energetic way, echoing the chants and colors that had already been associated with Olympiacos fans.

The ultras movement in Greece took on a life of its own, with both clubs' supporters forming close-knit communities that were bound not just by their love of football, but by their club's history, identity, and their place in Greek society. Rivalry chants, painted banners, and massive tifos (displays of banners and flags) became an integral part of the matchday atmosphere. The significance of the derby increased tenfold as both sides sought to outdo each other not just on the field, but in the stands as well.

The ultra culture surrounding the rivalry would soon spill out into other areas of Greek society, with fans sometimes clashing in the streets, creating a tense and dangerous environment. This fervor added to the intensity of the derby, ensuring that each encounter between Olympiacos and Panathinaikos would be more than just a match—it would be a battle of passion, pride, and an expression of the deep divides within Greek society.

Chapter 3: The First Major Clashes

The Early Iconic Matches and Their Significance

The rivalry between Olympiacos and Panathinaikos was born from more than just a competition between two football clubs; it was a contest of ideologies, pride, and identity. The first major clashes between the two clubs in the 1920s and 1930s laid the groundwork for what would become one of the fiercest rivalries in world football. While the games were, at the time, relatively low-key in terms of national attention, they carried an immense weight for the local fanbases.

In the early years, the encounters between Olympiacos and Panathinaikos were symbolic of the social and cultural divide that existed in Athens. These initial meetings were more than just matches; they were battles for local pride and supremacy. The importance of each derby grew over time, particularly as both clubs began to dominate Greek football. As both teams climbed the ranks of the Greek football league, their clashes began to attract wider attention. What had once been a local rivalry gradually became a national spectacle, marked by intensity on and off the pitch.

The first notable derby came in 1925, a year after Olympiacos' founding. While the match itself didn't have the same magnitude as later encounters, it marked the beginning of a legacy that would shape Greek football for decades to come. Olympiacos and Panathinaikos were still finding their footing as footballing institutions, but this game set the tone for the future. It was a hard-fought encounter with Olympiacos emerging victorious, a result that sparked early celebrations among their fans and began to instill a sense of superiority that would fuel their pride in the years to follow.

As the years progressed, the derbies became more intense. The 1930s and 1940s were characterized by more frequent encounters as both clubs started winning championships and making a name for themselves on the national stage. The matches, while still occasionally marked by harsh fouls and rough play, began to take on a more professional edge. Olympiacos and Panathinaikos had, by this time, established themselves as the two most successful clubs in Greek football, and each derby was now a contest not only for local pride but for the coveted title of national champion.

The significance of these early clashes lies in the foundation they laid for the future of Greek football. They showed the importance of the derby in Athens' social fabric, where football had become an outlet for political, social, and cultural expression. The early rivalries were not merely about footballing success; they symbolized the fierce competition between two worldviews and two sets of values.

A Look at the First Memorable Derby Victories

Although Olympiacos and Panathinaikos had both been successful in the early years of Greek football, the first truly memorable derby victories were crucial in shaping the identity of each club. These victories became milestones in their respective histories, reinforcing the clubs' philosophies and intensifying the rivalry that would only grow stronger in the decades to come.

One of the first memorable moments came in 1934, when Olympiacos defeated Panathinaikos in a decisive match that solidified their reputation as one of Greece's most formidable teams. While the match itself was not a championship decider, it was a victory that sent a strong message to Panathinaikos and their supporters. Olympiacos' 3-1 win was seen as a clear statement that they were not just a team from the working-class district of Piraeus, but a club with the talent and ambition to compete at the highest level. The celebration of this victory became emblematic of the Olympiacos spirit—a club that thrived on adversity and aimed to achieve success against the odds.

Panathinaikos, however, was not a club to take defeat lightly, and they responded with their own memorable derby moments. In 1940, Panathinaikos pulled off a historic victory over Olympiacos, defeating them 2-0 in front of a passionate crowd. This match remains etched in Panathinaikos' history as one of the great derby victories that helped solidify their status as Athens' elite football club. The result was not only a significant win on the pitch but also a reminder to Olympiacos that the battle for supremacy in Greek football would not be decided easily.

By the 1950s, the rivalry had reached new heights, with both teams constantly vying for the top spot in Greek football. Olympiacos and Panathinaikos were now locked in a fierce battle for dominance, and every derby carried the weight of history. One such match occurred in 1951, when Olympiacos triumphed in a 4-1 victory, a match that remains one of the most memorable in the club's early history. The victory was not only significant for its scoreline but also for its psychological impact, as it demonstrated Olympiacos' ability to dominate their rivals and showed that they were becoming the team to beat in Greek football.

For Panathinaikos, their own memorable derby victory came in 1965, a year when they claimed a 3-0 victory that became a symbol of their dominance at the time. The win not only strengthened their position as Greece's most prestigious club but also proved that they could outplay Olympiacos at their own game. The victory was celebrated by Panathinaikos supporters as a true representation of their superiority, and it provided a significant boost to the morale of the club's fanbase.

These early iconic victories set the tone for the future of the rivalry, demonstrating the fierce competitive nature that would define every encounter between Olympiacos and Panathinaikos. Each victory—whether it was Olympiacos' rise to prominence or Panathinaikos' quick resurgence—helped cultivate a sense of pride and identity that both clubs would carry with them for generations.

The results of these early matches also proved something far greater than just the final score: they showed that Greek football had become much more than a pastime. The derby had become a reflection of the larger social, cultural, and political dynamics of Greek life. It was a battleground for pride, identity, and the ever-present struggle for supremacy between Athens' two greatest footballing institutions.

Chapter 4: The Golden Eras: Successes and Struggles

Olympiacos' Domination in the 1990s and 2000s

The 1990s and 2000s were defining decades for Olympiacos, a period during which the club solidified its dominance in Greek football, establishing itself as the clear leader of the domestic league. By the time the 1990s arrived, Olympiacos had already built a reputation as a competitive and ambitious club, but it was during this time that they began to assert their superiority over Panathinaikos in both Greek football and European competitions.

Under the guidance of legendary coaches like Vangelis Vlachos and later, the influential Dutch tactician Leo Beenhakker, Olympiacos not only continued their domestic dominance but also began to take Greek football into the international spotlight. The 1990s marked the beginning of a golden era where Olympiacos started to dominate the Greek Super League, clinching multiple league titles throughout the decade.

In 1997, Olympiacos made history by winning their first Greek championship in eight years. This victory was not just a return to the top, but a statement of intent. The club built a reputation on a combination of fiery passion, tactical discipline, and a relentless pursuit of excellence. With players like Giorgos Karagounis, who later became a symbol of Greek football, Olympiacos were a force to be reckoned with. But it wasn't just Karagounis; the club also boasted a number of foreign stars who added to the team's star power. This period saw Olympiacos firmly cement its place as the team to beat in Greece, and their consistent success in the 2000s further solidified their status as the most successful Greek club in terms of titles.

The pinnacle of Olympiacos' success came in 2004 when they secured a remarkable five consecutive league titles under coach Takis Lemonis. This era marked a period of unrivaled success, during which Olympiacos' dominance was unmatched. The club also made impressive strides in European football, consistently qualifying for the group stages of the UEFA Champions League, a competition they had long struggled to make a significant mark in. The period from 1997 to 2009 was the height of Olympiacos' modern-day supremacy, with the club winning the Greek league title on several occasions, reasserting themselves as the dominant force in Greek football.

Panathinaikos' Rise and Periods of Dominance

While Olympiacos enjoyed an era of dominance in the 1990s and 2000s, Panathinaikos was not to be outdone. The club had experienced its own moments of glory in the earlier decades, but it was in the late 2000s that Panathinaikos began to rise again, challenging Olympiacos for supremacy both domestically and on the international stage.

The early 2000s were a time of transition for Panathinaikos. While Olympiacos was lifting league titles, Panathinaikos was focused on rebuilding and strengthening their squad. After several years of relative struggle, the 2004–2005 season marked the beginning of a new chapter for the club. Under the management of Fernando Santos, Panathinaikos began to assert itself as a serious contender once more. The team was built on a foundation of solid defending, an organized midfield, and a forward line capable of scoring goals. In 2004, Panathinaikos won the Greek Cup, and in 2006, they were crowned champions of Greece once again, ending a three-year title drought. This victory was particularly sweet for Panathinaikos fans, as it was achieved in a season where Olympiacos appeared to be unstoppable.

Panathinaikos' resurgence continued into the late 2000s, with the club not only competing strongly in the Greek league but also making their mark in European competitions. The 2008–2009 season was especially significant for Panathinaikos, as they reached the quarterfinals of the UEFA Champions League, a feat that had not been accomplished in over a decade. Although the team did not win the competition, their progress was an indication of the club's return to prominence.

By the 2010s, Panathinaikos had reclaimed its place as one of Greece's most successful and influential football clubs, once again competing for league titles and regaining their respectability on the European stage. However, despite their resurgence, they faced a number of challenges in the coming years, both on and off the pitch. Financial issues and internal struggles would eventually take their toll, but the late 2000s and early 2010s remain a period where Panathinaikos challenged Olympiacos for supremacy in a way that had not been seen since the early decades of the rivalry.

Key Players That Defined Each Club's Golden Era

Throughout their respective golden eras, Olympiacos and Panathinaikos were defined by certain players whose performances and leadership became synonymous with success. These footballing legends not only helped to shape the trajectory of their clubs but also played a crucial role in ensuring that their teams remained at the top of Greek football.

For Olympiacos, players like Rivaldo, the Brazilian maestro who joined the club in 2004, were central to their success. Rivaldo's creativity, vision, and flair on the ball made him a fan favorite and a driving force behind Olympiacos' rise in the 2000s. His presence was not just symbolic of Olympiacos' ambition but also provided the club with an international superstar who could compete at the highest level. Alongside Rivaldo, players like Angelos Charisteas, who played a key role in Greece's 2004 UEFA Euro triumph, brought experience and grit to the squad. Meanwhile, Greek players like Giorgos Karagounis, Vassilis Tsartas, and the legendary club captain, Giannis Maniatis, were the backbone of the Olympiacos midfield, providing energy, leadership, and determination in every match.

On the Panathinaikos side, the late 1990s and early 2000s saw the emergence of some of the most talented players in Greek football. Players like Giorgos Karagounis, who later moved to Olympiacos but was initially a key figure at Panathinaikos, were at the heart of the team's midfield. Karagounis' ability to dictate play, his vision, and his leadership made him a symbol of the club during its period of success. Another standout player for Panathinaikos during this period was the forward Angelos Charisteas, whose goalscoring abilities made him one of Greece's most lethal attackers. The combination of domestic talent and international stars such as Serbian forward Savo Milošević helped Panathinaikos compete at the highest level and challenged Olympiacos' dominance in the Greek league.

These key players, along with others, provided the fuel for both clubs' golden eras. Their contributions on the field shaped not only the fortunes of their teams but also the fabric of the derby itself. Their brilliance, skill, and leadership ensured that both Olympiacos and Panathinaikos would remain at the heart of Greek football for years to come, further intensifying the rivalry that continues to captivate fans across Greece and beyond.

Chapter 5: The Role of the Fans

Understanding the Ultras Culture of Both Clubs

The role of the fans in the rivalry between Olympiacos and Panathinaikos cannot be overstated. The passion, energy, and dedication of both sets of supporters have become synonymous with the derby itself. However, it is the ultras culture that has become the most visible and defining element of the supporters' identities, adding a unique and intense dimension to the rivalry.

At the heart of Olympiacos' fan culture is the infamous "Gate 7" ultras group. Known for their fiery passion and unwavering support, Gate 7 represents the heart and soul of the Olympiacos fanbase. Founded in 1987, the group quickly became a formidable presence in Greek football, not only supporting the team in the stands but also playing a significant role in creating an intimidating atmosphere at every Olympiacos match, especially during the derby against Panathinaikos. Gate 7's presence is marked by their passionate chants, huge banners, and the ever-present sea of red and white flags. Their support goes beyond just football; it is an expression of their loyalty to the club, the city of Piraeus, and the working-class values that Olympiacos embodies. For Olympiacos fans, their love for the club is woven deeply into their personal identities, and Gate

7 has become a symbol of the club's fierce determination to stand firm in the face of opposition.

On the other side of the rivalry, Panathinaikos supporters have their own ultras group, the "Gate 13" fans. Established in the early 1980s, Gate 13 quickly became a symbol of Panathinaikos' own passionate following. As with Olympiacos' Gate 7, Panathinaikos' ultras are known for their relentless support, vivid displays of banners and flags, and chants that echo through the stands. However, there is a distinct difference in their culture. While Olympiacos' fans often have an aggressive and rowdy edge, Panathinaikos supporters pride themselves on their tradition and their connection to the intellectual and cultural identity of Athens. For Panathinaikos, supporting the club is not just about football; it is a manifestation of their sense of pride in the team's rich history and their role as the "elite" of Athens. Gate 13's presence is marked by a strong sense of camaraderie, with supporters viewing their loyalty as a reflection of their loyalty to Panathinaikos' ideals.

The ultras culture at both clubs is not just about supporting their teams in football matches; it is a lifestyle. For many fans, it extends far beyond the pitch and shapes their lives off it. This intense dedication to the club creates an atmosphere where emotions run high, and every match, especially the derby, is seen as a personal battle. The feeling of belonging to an organized fan group gives supporters a sense of purpose and pride, making every encounter with Panathinaikos or Olympiacos an event that goes far beyond just three points.

The Significance of the Supporters' Rivalry

The rivalry between Olympiacos and Panathinaikos is not confined to the football field. The significance of the supporters' rivalry has far-reaching implications, affecting not only the two clubs but also the wider Greek society. The stakes of the derby are much higher than simply who wins the match; they are about pride, identity, and a sense of belonging. For the fans, these derbies become a platform for expressing their emotions, their frustrations, and their desires to assert dominance over the other.

The rivalry extends beyond the matchday atmosphere. It is a social, political, and cultural war between the two fanbases, with each set of supporters looking to prove their superiority not just in football but in every other area of Greek life. Olympiacos fans, often seen as the voice of the working-class and the heart of Piraeus, believe they are the true embodiment of the city's spirit. Panathinaikos supporters, representing the intellectual and more cosmopolitan side of Athens, view their club as a symbol of class, tradition, and excellence. These deep cultural and social divides amplify the intensity of the derby, turning what could be just another football match into a battle for the soul of Athens.

For both sets of supporters, winning the derby is about more than just football. It is about asserting their place in Greek society, showcasing the strength of their community, and reaffirming their identity. The rivalry is not only about the success of the team; it is a representation of who they are as individuals and the values they hold dear. Olympiacos and Panathinaikos fans view the derby as a representation of their wider struggle for recognition, making every win feel like a victory for their beliefs and way of life.

This rivalry is deeply embedded in the culture of Greek football and society. The fanbases are constantly at odds, both in terms of their approach to football and their broader views on life. It is a rivalry that transcends the football field, playing out in daily conversations, social gatherings, and even in political discourse. The derby has become a manifestation of the deep-seated divides in Greek society, with each side fighting to prove that their worldview is the superior one.

Famous Fan Incidents and Violence Tied to the Derby

Unfortunately, the intensity of the rivalry between Olympiacos and Panathinaikos has often spilled over into violence. The passion of both fanbases can sometimes take a dark turn, leading to violent clashes both inside and outside the stadium. These incidents have become a significant part of the derby's history, tarnishing the beauty of the rivalry and reminding everyone of the dangers of unchecked passion.

One of the most notorious incidents occurred in 1980, when violence erupted before and during a derby match at the Olympic Stadium. Tensions were already high between the two fanbases, and what was meant to be a showcase of Greek football turned into a nightmarish scene. Fans from both clubs clashed in the streets surrounding the stadium, resulting in injuries and arrests. The match itself was marred by violent altercations, and it marked the beginning of a period of increased tension in the rivalry.

Another infamous incident occurred in 2007, when Olympiacos supporters clashed with police during a high-stakes derby. The match, which was played at Olympiacos' home ground, Karaiskakis Stadium, saw violent confrontations both inside and outside the stadium. Riot police were called to restore order as fights broke out between rival fans. This clash was not just a result of the match itself but was fueled by years of pent-up frustration, with each fanbase growing increasingly hostile toward the other.

In more recent years, the violence surrounding the derby has continued, though it has become less frequent due to increased security measures and police presence at matches. However, the threat of violence remains ever-present, and both clubs have had to take steps to manage the behavior of their fanbases. The Greek government, as well as the clubs themselves, have worked to curb the violence, but the history of clashes remains a significant part of the derby's narrative.

The role of the fans in the Olympiacos-Panathinaikos rivalry is one of passion, identity, and, unfortunately, sometimes violence. The ultras culture at both clubs has created a fierce, unwavering support for the team, but it has also given rise to dangerous incidents that have marred the beauty of the game. Yet, despite these moments of conflict, the rivalry between Olympiacos and Panathinaikos continues to be one of the most exciting and intense in world football, fueled by the undying passion of their fans.

Chapter 6: Key Moments in the Derby's History

Decisive Wins and Defeats

The Olympiacos-Panathinaikos rivalry is a tapestry woven with moments of glory and despair. Through the decades, there have been decisive wins and crushing defeats, all of which have added layers of intensity to an already fierce rivalry. Each victory and loss is more than just a result; it's a defining chapter in the story of Greek football.

One of the most decisive wins in the derby's history came in 1995, when Olympiacos triumphed over Panathinaikos with a 3-0 victory that left a lasting imprint on both teams. This match was significant not just for the scoreline but for the way Olympiacos dominated the game. It was a resounding statement of intent, showing that Olympiacos was the team to beat in Greek football. The loss was a bitter blow for Panathinaikos, who had prided themselves on their dominance in Greek football during the 1980s and early 1990s. The match marked the start of a new era, with Olympiacos firmly establishing themselves as the dominant force in Greek football for the years that followed.

For Panathinaikos, one of the most defining victories came in 2004 when they clinched a 2-1 win over

Olympiacos in a match that was crucial to the team's season. The victory not only handed Panathinaikos a much-needed three points in their pursuit of the league title but also served as a symbol of their resilience after years of Olympiacos dominance. The match was filled with drama, with Panathinaikos securing the win in the final minutes, sending their fans into raptures and signaling that the power shift in Greek football was far from over. It was a victory that rekindled the hope and pride of Panathinaikos fans, who saw their team as once again capable of challenging Olympiacos' supremacy.

However, one of the most memorable defeats in the rivalry came in 2007, when Olympiacos delivered a crushing 4-0 defeat to Panathinaikos. The match was an absolute demolition, one of the most dominant performances ever witnessed in the history of the derby. Olympiacos' superiority was on full display as they overwhelmed Panathinaikos with attacking football and clinical finishing. The defeat left Panathinaikos reeling, and while they had been competitive in many recent derbies, this loss was a clear reminder that Olympiacos was still the team to beat. For Olympiacos fans, the victory was a statement that their club was the preeminent force in Greek football.

Matches That Have Defined the Rivalry

There are certain matches in the history of the Olympiacos-Panathinaikos derby that have come to define the rivalry. These games are not just about the final score; they represent pivotal moments that have shaped the trajectory of both clubs and the nature of the derby itself.

One such match took place in 1969, when Panathinaikos faced Olympiacos in a contest that would go down in history. Panathinaikos won 3-2 in a game that epitomized everything that made the rivalry so intense. This encounter saw dramatic twists and turns, with Olympiacos taking an early lead before Panathinaikos mounted a thrilling comeback. The victory was pivotal in ensuring Panathinaikos' dominance in the late 1960s, and it cemented their status as one of the top footballing institutions in Greece. It also represented the ongoing struggle for supremacy between the two teams, with each side fighting tooth and nail for victory.

Another defining moment came in 1997 when Olympiacos won 3-1 against Panathinaikos in what would become known as the "Battle of the Piraeus." The match was physical and aggressive, with both teams giving their all in front of a packed stadium. Olympiacos' victory was a watershed moment, as they emerged as the dominant force in Greek football at the time. The match was significant not only for the scoreline but also for the way Olympiacos asserted their physicality and mental toughness over their rivals. It marked a shift in the balance of power in the derby and set the stage for Olympiacos' dominance in the following decades.

Perhaps one of the most memorable encounters came in 2000, when Panathinaikos secured a 2-0 victory at home, in front of a raucous crowd at the Olympic Stadium. The match was filled with tension, and the win was crucial in Panathinaikos' pursuit of the league title that season. The victory was a testament to the resilience of the team, as they managed to overcome Olympiacos in a fiercely contested match. The win helped Panathinaikos regain their footing as a serious contender for the title and gave their supporters a long-awaited moment of triumph over their bitter rivals.

Unforgettable Moments in the History of the Games

While the decisive victories and defining matches have shaped the history of the Olympiacos-Panathinaikos derby, it is the unforgettable moments—both on and off the pitch—that have truly defined this legendary rivalry.

One such moment came in 2004, during a dramatic late-game winner from Panathinaikos' Angelos Charisteas in the dying minutes of a 2-1 win over Olympiacos. Charisteas, a hero for both Panathinaikos and Greece's 2004 European Championship-winning team, scored a goal that would forever be etched in the memories of Panathinaikos supporters. The roar that followed the goal was deafening, and the euphoria of the moment carried a special weight, as it not only handed Panathinaikos the three points but also signaled their return to the summit of Greek football. For Olympiacos, the loss was a bitter one, made even more painful by the timing of the goal, which seemed to come at the peak of their hopes for another league title.

Another unforgettable moment took place in 1995, when Olympiacos' Giorgos Karagounis scored a spectacular long-range goal that remains one of the most iconic goals in derby history. The goal, which gave Olympiacos a 2-0 lead, was a testament to Karagounis' brilliance, and it left the Panathinaikos defenders and goalkeeper with no chance. The goal became a symbol of Olympiacos' skill and determination, and for many fans, it encapsulated the essence of their club's approach to the derby: aggressive, relentless, and always striving for victory.

Off the pitch, one of the most unforgettable moments came in 2007 when both sets of fans clashed violently in the streets after a derby match. The violence that followed the game shocked Greece, and it became a stark reminder of how deeply the rivalry ran. While such incidents are a dark chapter in the history of the derby, they serve as a testament to the intensity of the emotions tied to the match. The atmosphere surrounding these games is often so charged with passion that it spills over into the streets, underscoring the deep social, cultural, and political divides that exist between the two clubs' supporters.

For both sets of fans, the derby is far more than just a football match; it is an event that touches every part of their lives, and every encounter is laden with significance. From the goals to the tackles, from the celebrations to the confrontations, these moments are what make the Olympiacos-Panathinaikos derby one of the most thrilling and emotional fixtures in world football.

Chapter 7: The Managers' Influence

How Coaches Have Shaped the Rivalry

While the players on the field have always been the focal point of the Olympiacos vs. Panathinaikos rivalry, the managers who have guided these clubs have had an equally significant impact on the competition's intensity and direction. The influence of coaches in shaping the rivalry goes far beyond the tactical decisions they make; their leadership, approach to team-building, and ability to motivate players have all played a pivotal role in defining the historic encounters between the two clubs.

Coaches often bring with them distinct styles, philosophies, and mindsets, which influence how their teams approach the derby. For both Olympiacos and Panathinaikos, the tactical battles on derby day are as important as the emotional stakes. The results of these games frequently reflect not just individual brilliance on the field but also the strategic planning and psychological preparation from the men leading the teams from the sidelines.

In a rivalry as fierce as the one between Olympiacos and Panathinaikos, managers become symbols of their respective clubs, embodying their team's identity and values. The emotional intensity of the derby is often heightened by the strategic decisions made by the coaches, with each tactical move scrutinized, analyzed, and discussed by both sets of fans. Managers are often judged not only by their success in the derby but also by how they are able to mentally and physically prepare their teams for one of the most challenging fixtures in Greek football.

Iconic Managers Who Have Guided Each Club

Throughout the history of the rivalry, there have been several iconic managers who have become synonymous with either Olympiacos or Panathinaikos, guiding them to glory and shaping their destinies.

For Olympiacos, one of the most influential figures was the Dutch coach Leo Beenhakker. Beenhakker, who took charge of Olympiacos in the late 1990s, helped elevate the club's status in European football. His tenure was marked by a highly disciplined tactical approach, with a focus on structured defensive play and efficient counter-attacks. Beenhakker's Olympiacos teams were known for their tactical consistency, which helped the club secure multiple Greek league titles. His leadership during the 1999–2000 season, in particular, was critical in Olympiacos' quest for dominance, and his ability to inspire his team against fierce rivals like Panathinaikos was a hallmark of his time at the club.

Another important figure in the history of Olympiacos was Takis Lemonis, who took over in the early 2000s and guided the club to multiple championships. Lemonis was a pragmatic coach known for his no-nonsense approach to management. He emphasized team cohesion and work ethic, and under his leadership, Olympiacos enjoyed a period of sustained success. His calm demeanor and ability to motivate his players during high-pressure moments—especially in derbies—became a defining characteristic of his tenure. Lemonis' Olympiacos side was clinical and efficient, qualities that made them formidable opponents in the Greek league and the derby against Panathinaikos.

For Panathinaikos, one of the most notable and successful managers was the Portuguese tactician Fernando Santos. Santos took the reins in the early 2000s and helped restore the club to its former glory. His emphasis on disciplined defensive organization, combined with a powerful attacking style, revitalized Panathinaikos and led them to domestic success. Santos' influence extended beyond the Greek borders, as he guided Panathinaikos to the quarterfinals of the UEFA Champions League in 2009—a landmark achievement for the club. His ability to manage the pressures of the Olympiacos derby, keeping his team focused and motivated, was key to his success.

Another legendary figure for Panathinaikos was the Greek coach, Giannis Patros. Patros, a former player for the club, understood the deep cultural significance of the derby. His passion and connection to the club's rich history allowed him to communicate that same intensity to his players. Patros was also a master tactician, often using an aggressive pressing game that caught Olympiacos off guard during crucial moments. Under his leadership, Panathinaikos was able to challenge Olympiacos' dominance and deliver some memorable victories in the derby, including their 2-0 triumph in 2000, which remains one of the most significant wins in recent memory.

Tactical Battles in the Derby

The tactical battles in the Olympiacos vs. Panathinaikos derby have often been as intense and captivating as the matches themselves. Managers' approaches to the game can determine the outcome of these high-stakes encounters, and the strategic decisions made on the sidelines often come to define the derby's legacy.

One of the most crucial aspects of the tactical battles has been the differing styles of play between the two teams. Olympiacos, traditionally known for their high-pressing game, often looked to dominate possession and impose their physicality on the match. In contrast, Panathinaikos has frequently favored a more patient, possession-based style of football, relying on quick passing and technical precision to break down their opponents. These contrasting philosophies have created fascinating encounters, with managers constantly adapting their tactics to gain the upper hand.

During the 1990s and 2000s, under Beenhakker and Lemonis, Olympiacos developed a tactical approach that focused on creating compact defensive units, with an emphasis on counter-attacking football. Olympiacos' ability to transition quickly from defense to attack, using the pace of players like Rivaldo and Angelos Charisteas, made them a dangerous side, particularly in the derby. Olympiacos' managers often employed a 4-4-2 or 4-3-3 formation, designed to ensure a solid defensive base while giving their attacking players the freedom to express themselves on the counter.

In contrast, Panathinaikos under Santos was known for their well-organized defense and fluid midfield play. Santos often used a 4-3-3 or 4-2-3-1 formation, relying on players like Giorgos Karagounis to dictate the tempo in midfield. The tactical battle in the derby often revolved around how well Panathinaikos could control possession and break through Olympiacos' defensive lines. Santos emphasized maintaining discipline and keeping possession, trying to force Olympiacos into mistakes before launching quick attacks. Panathinaikos' success in the derby often came down to their ability to execute these tactics under pressure, using creativity and flair to outplay their rivals.

Another tactical battle that has defined the derby is the management of key moments. In several derbies, both Olympiacos and Panathinaikos have gone into the second half with one goal down, and the tactical changes made during the break have proved to be pivotal. For instance, managers like Lemonis and Santos were known to make bold decisions, switching up formations or making crucial substitutions, that could swing the momentum of the match in their favor.

The derby has often been a reflection of the tactical acumen of the managers involved. Whether through direct and physical play, patient buildup, or sudden bursts of attacking brilliance, each manager's strategy has been tested to the limit in one of football's most intense rivalries. In these high-pressure games, it is often the manager who can remain calm, think strategically, and adapt on the fly who comes out on top. And for the fans, the tactical decisions and the execution of those strategies are as much a part of the derby's drama as the goals and the wins themselves.

Chapter 8: The International Stage: Olympiacos and Panathinaikos in European Competitions

Successes and Failures in European Football

The Olympiacos vs. Panathinaikos rivalry extends far beyond the confines of domestic Greek football; it has also been shaped by the clubs' performances in European competitions. Both clubs have enjoyed success on the international stage, yet their fortunes in European football have been markedly different, adding yet another layer of intensity to their domestic rivalry.

For Olympiacos, the 1990s and 2000s marked the club's ascent to prominence in European football. Olympiacos' ability to compete consistently in the UEFA Champions League and the UEFA Europa League was a testament to the club's financial strength and its growing reputation as a footballing powerhouse in Greece. Their most notable European achievement came in the 1999-2000 season, when they reached the quarterfinals of the UEFA Champions League—a remarkable achievement for a club with relatively limited resources compared to the giants of European football. The club's campaign that year was marked by memorable victories, including a win over English giants Arsenal, which highlighted

Olympiacos' ability to mix defensive solidity with attacking flair.

Throughout the 2000s, Olympiacos' consistent participation in the group stages of the Champions League became a symbol of their dominance in Greece. While they were often unable to advance far in the competition, their ability to qualify for the prestigious tournament year after year showcased the club's strength. Olympiacos also found success in the UEFA Europa League, where they reached the Round of 16 multiple times and occasionally made deep runs into the competition. The club's performances in Europe helped solidify their identity as Greece's most successful club on the international stage.

Panathinaikos, on the other hand, has enjoyed periods of extraordinary success in Europe, but they have also faced their share of disappointments. The pinnacle of Panathinaikos' European achievement came in 1971 when they reached the final of the European Cup (now the UEFA Champions League). Though they were defeated by Ajax in the final, Panathinaikos' journey to the championship match remains one of the greatest achievements in Greek football history. Their run to the final that year was a testament to their skill and ambition, and it elevated the club to international prominence.

In the 2000s, Panathinaikos enjoyed a resurgence in European competitions under the guidance of coach Fernando Santos. The highlight came in the 2008-2009 UEFA Champions League season when Panathinaikos reached the quarterfinals. This was an impressive achievement, considering the level of competition in the tournament. Panathinaikos' victory over European giants like Manchester City and Villarreal in the knockout stages proved their resilience and tactical discipline. Despite falling short of winning major European titles, Panathinaikos' continued success in Europe—especially during the late 2000s—cemented their status as a club that could compete with the best.

However, both clubs have also had their fair share of European disappointments. Olympiacos, despite their consistent appearances in the Champions League, have often struggled to progress past the group stages, facing challenges against Europe's elite clubs. Similarly, Panathinaikos' periodic exits from European competitions, often in the group stages or early knockout rounds, have highlighted the gap in quality between Greece's top clubs and the powerhouses of Europe.

How International Competitions Have Added to the Rivalry

While domestic matches between Olympiacos and Panathinaikos are the heart of their rivalry, their performances in European competitions have added another dimension to the rivalry. European football provides a larger stage, where both clubs can measure themselves against the best teams on the continent. For the fans, seeing their team compete at the highest level of European football has become a matter of immense pride, and each European success adds to the narrative of the rivalry.

The international success of both clubs has intensified the rivalry by giving them more opportunities to one-up each other. Each time one club has a successful European campaign, the other feels the pressure to match or exceed that achievement. Olympiacos' consistent appearances in the Champions League, for instance, have placed the club in direct competition with Panathinaikos in terms of European stature. While Olympiacos may have had the upper hand domestically, Panathinaikos' success in Europe has been a constant reminder that their rivalry goes beyond Greece.

The sense of superiority in European football has become another way for fans to measure the success of their club. For Olympiacos fans, European competition is a chance to assert that their club is the dominant force in Greek football, not just on a domestic level but internationally. For Panathinaikos, each memorable victory in Europe is a reminder of their historical legacy and their ability to compete with the best, a message to their rivals that they are far more than just domestic champions.

Moreover, European football has allowed both clubs to showcase their passion on a grander stage. The atmosphere in Olympiacos' Karaiskakis Stadium or Panathinaikos' Olympic Stadium during European nights is electric, with both sets of supporters turning out in full force. These matches are not just about football; they are a celebration of the club's identity and their place in European football. The stakes are higher, and the passion is even more intense, as each team seeks to prove their worth on the international stage.

Memorable European Nights Involving the Two Clubs

Some of the most unforgettable moments in the history of the Olympiacos-Panathinaikos rivalry have occurred in European competitions, where the clubs have faced off against not just their domestic rivals but also some of the best teams in the world.

One of the most iconic moments came in 2009, when Panathinaikos faced off against Olympiacos in a fiercely contested Champions League qualifier. The two teams, having already established themselves as the titans of Greek football, met on the European stage, with both sets of supporters fully aware of the significance of the clash. The match was not just a battle for three points but a chance to prove which club truly held the upper hand in Greek football, both domestically and internationally. Panathinaikos won the match 1-0, a result that sent a wave of celebration through the fanbase and reinforced their reputation as a club capable of performing under pressure, even in the most challenging of circumstances.

Another unforgettable European night came in 2004, when Olympiacos secured a famous 3-1 victory over Arsenal in the Champions League. Olympiacos' ability to defeat a team of Arsenal's caliber in front of their own fans sent shockwaves through European football. This victory was a crowning moment for Olympiacos, proving that they could compete with the best and that their European aspirations were not just pipe dreams. The match was a testament to Olympiacos' growing strength and their ability to perform on the big stage.

The rivalry also reached new heights during the 1999-2000 UEFA Champions League, when Olympiacos faced off against Panathinaikos in a gripping encounter. The match had all the ingredients of a classic derby—high stakes, passionate fans, and a European backdrop that made the game even more significant. Olympiacos won the match 2-1, which added another layer of intensity to the rivalry. The fact that it was played on the international stage only heightened the tension, and the result left both sets of fans with plenty to talk about for years to come.

These European nights, whether they resulted in victory or defeat, have contributed to the enduring nature of the Olympiacos-Panathinaikos rivalry. They have elevated the stakes, provided moments of history, and reminded everyone that the competition between these two clubs extends far beyond Greece. The international stage has given their rivalry a global audience and solidified their places as two of the most iconic clubs in European football.

Chapter 9: Controversies and Scandals

Referee Decisions That Changed the Course of Derbies

In a rivalry as fierce and passionate as the one between Olympiacos and Panathinaikos, controversies and scandals are inevitable. The emotional intensity of the derby often amplifies every decision made on the pitch, especially those involving referees. Over the years, several controversial refereeing decisions have become infamous for their impact on the outcome of the derby, further fueling the animosity between the two clubs and their supporters.

One of the most talked-about incidents occurred in 2007 during a dramatic 2-2 draw at Karaiskakis Stadium. Olympiacos were leading 2-1 with just minutes remaining when Panathinaikos were awarded a dubious penalty after a challenge in the box that many believed was not deserving of a spot-kick. The referee's decision was met with fierce protests from Olympiacos players and fans, who felt that the penalty was a gift to their rivals. Panathinaikos converted the penalty, earning a last-minute draw, and the result left Olympiacos supporters feeling aggrieved. The controversy surrounding the penalty was amplified by accusations of bias and a belief that the referee's decision had unfairly altered the outcome of the match. For Panathinaikos fans, however, it was a well-deserved point—a symbol of their resilience and ability to fight back, even when things weren't going their way.

Another infamous moment came in 2012, when Olympiacos were awarded a penalty in a match at the Olympic Stadium. The decision came under heavy scrutiny after a questionable foul in the penalty area, with many believing the referee had made an error in judgment. Panathinaikos fans were enraged by the call, accusing the referee of favoring Olympiacos and handing them an unfair advantage. The controversy surrounding the penalty fueled heated debates in the media and among fans, and the incident became one of the most talked-about moments in recent derby history.

These controversial referee decisions have often overshadowed the football itself, adding fuel to the already tense atmosphere surrounding the derby. For both sets of fans, these moments are seen as part of a broader narrative of injustice and perceived favoritism, whether for or against their respective clubs. In a rivalry where every match feels like a battle for pride, even the smallest decision can spark outrage, and the role of referees in these high-stakes encounters is constantly under scrutiny.

Controversial Moments in Derby Matches

Over the years, there have been several controversial moments in Olympiacos vs. Panathinaikos derbies that have added to the drama and legacy of the rivalry. These moments, whether on the pitch or off it, have become part of the folklore of the fixture, defining how both clubs and their supporters view the derby.

One such moment came in 1999 when Olympiacos and Panathinaikos faced off in a tense match that ended with Olympiacos' 2-1 victory. The match was full of drama, but it was a specific incident involving a hard tackle by Panathinaikos' defender that sparked outrage. The tackle was deemed by many as dangerous and reckless, and it led to a confrontation between players from both sides. The intensity of the challenge and the subsequent altercation between the two teams highlighted the aggressive nature of the derby, but it also fueled the notion that these games often went beyond football into the realm of personal battles. The incident was one of many where the heat of the moment boiled over, leading to tempers flaring and creating a charged atmosphere both on and off the pitch.

In the 2004-2005 season, a clash between Olympiacos and Panathinaikos at the Olympic Stadium became infamous for an altercation between players and coaching staff. As the match reached its final stages, tensions escalated after a controversial goal by Olympiacos was allowed to stand, despite claims from Panathinaikos that the ball had gone out of play before being crossed into the penalty area. The referee's decision caused uproar among Panathinaikos players, who protested vehemently. The dispute quickly spiraled into a verbal altercation between the two teams, with coaching staff and substitutes getting involved in the heated exchange. The incident further fueled the narrative of injustice and bias in the rivalry, with Panathinaikos supporters claiming that the officiating had cost them the match. The post-match fallout was filled with accusations and allegations, leaving a bitter taste in the mouths of both fans and players alike.

The physicality of the derby has also led to controversial moments over the years. In 2000, a match at the Olympic Stadium saw a brutal challenge by Olympiacos' midfielder against Panathinaikos' key player, Mimis Domazos. The tackle was harsh and resulted in Domazos being forced off the field with an injury, leading to furious protests from Panathinaikos fans. The incident sparked a debate about the level of aggression allowed in the derby and the role of referees in controlling the match. Olympiacos fans, on the other hand, defended the tackle as part of the hard-nosed approach their team often employed, especially in such a high-stakes match.

These controversial moments have only added to the intensity of the rivalry, with each team's supporters using these incidents to fuel their belief that the other team is given unfair advantages. For fans of both Olympiacos and Panathinaikos, these events become more than just incidents; they are part of the broader narrative of a rivalry that has shaped the culture of Greek football.

The Political Aspect of the Rivalry

The Olympiacos vs. Panathinaikos derby has never been solely about football. Over the years, the rivalry has taken on a deeper, more political dimension, with both clubs representing competing ideologies and social classes in Greek society. The cultural divide between the working-class areas of Piraeus, where Olympiacos is based, and the more affluent areas of Athens, where Panathinaikos is located, has played a crucial role in shaping the political undertones of the rivalry.

Olympiacos, representing the working-class districts of Piraeus, has long been associated with the left-wing and socialist movements in Greece. The club's fans, many of whom identify with the struggles of the working class, have often expressed their political views in the context of their support for Olympiacos. Over the years, Olympiacos' ultras have frequently used the stadium as a platform to voice their political beliefs, with chants and banners supporting left-wing causes. This political dimension adds another layer of tension to the rivalry, as Panathinaikos supporters, who are often associated with more conservative and right-wing ideologies, view Olympiacos' political stance as a direct challenge to their values.

On the other hand, Panathinaikos has long been linked with the political and intellectual elite of Athens, who have traditionally supported more conservative ideologies. The club's supporters, who are seen as representing the higher classes, have often clashed with Olympiacos' working-class fanbase, both on and off the field. In the context of the derby, these political and class-based divides add to the intensity of the competition, with each side not just fighting for victory but also for their vision of Greek society and their place within it.

The political element of the rivalry is not limited to the stands, however. It has also spilled over into the boardrooms of both clubs, where political affiliations have often played a role in shaping the direction of the teams. The involvement of wealthy and politically influential figures in both clubs has sometimes led to accusations of corruption and favoritism, further fueling the belief that the derby is more than just a sporting event; it is a microcosm of the broader political and social struggles in Greece.

The political aspect of the rivalry has also extended to the media, with journalists and commentators often framing the matches in terms of class, ideology, and national identity. For Olympiacos fans, the rivalry represents a battle for the rights and recognition of the working class, while for Panathinaikos supporters, it is a struggle to defend the traditions and values of the intellectual elite. The political tension that underpins the rivalry has made the derby a fixture that transcends football, with each game representing a wider battle for control over the cultural and political narrative of Greece.

Chapter 10: The Modern-Day Rivalry

How the Rivalry Has Evolved in the Current Era

The Olympiacos vs. Panathinaikos derby has always been about more than just football; it is a cultural event that encapsulates the very essence of Greek footballing identity. In the modern era, this rivalry has evolved, becoming both more competitive and more commercialized, while still retaining the fierce passion and historical significance that have defined it for over a century.

In recent years, the derby has become a clash not just of two football clubs, but of two different approaches to footballing success. Olympiacos, with its financial strength and consistent dominance of the Greek Super League, has remained a force in both domestic and European competitions. The club's ability to regularly qualify for the UEFA Champions League group stages and its strength in the league have made them the benchmark for success in Greek football. Olympiacos' continued dominance has put them at the forefront of Greek football, and their ability to attract top-tier foreign players has helped them stay competitive on the international stage.

Panathinaikos, while still one of Greece's most successful clubs, has faced more challenges in recent years. The club has struggled to maintain the same level of financial stability that Olympiacos has enjoyed, leading to a period of rebuilding and restructuring. Despite this, Panathinaikos has managed to maintain a competitive edge, often relying on homegrown talent and young players to compete in the domestic league. Their success in the derby has become less frequent, but the desire to reclaim their position as Greece's top club remains strong, particularly when facing their bitter rivals. The changes in both clubs have given the modern-day derby a different flavor, with Olympiacos frequently being seen as the dominant side, while Panathinaikos continues to fight back, motivated by the history and pride of their club.

While the rivalry has evolved in terms of the on-field action, the passion and fervor of both fanbases have remained unchanged. The stadiums are still packed with passionate supporters, the chants and songs echoing through the stands, and the atmosphere is as charged as ever. The modern-day rivalry still carries the weight of history, but it also reflects the changes in the footballing landscape, both in Greece and beyond.

The Financial Implications and the Role of Foreign Players

The financial dynamics of Greek football have played a crucial role in shaping the modern-day rivalry between Olympiacos and Panathinaikos. Olympiacos, with its significant financial backing and investment, has been able to maintain a competitive advantage over their rivals. The club's financial strength has allowed them to attract some of the best foreign players to Greece, which in turn has helped them remain competitive in both domestic and international competitions.

Olympiacos' ability to bring in top-tier foreign talent has been key to their dominance in the Greek league. The club's scouting network and financial resources have enabled them to sign high-profile players from countries like Brazil, Spain, and Africa, bolstering their squad and giving them the edge in terms of talent. Players such as Valbuena, Manduca, and Pardo have brought invaluable experience and technical ability to Olympiacos, and their presence in the team has played a pivotal role in maintaining the club's winning culture. The financial power of Olympiacos has allowed them to build a squad capable of competing at the highest level, both in Greece and Europe.

In contrast, Panathinaikos has faced significant financial challenges over the past decade, which have impacted their ability to sign foreign players of the same caliber. The club's struggles to secure sponsorships and maintain financial stability have led to a reliance on homegrown talent and younger, less experienced players. While Panathinaikos has continued to produce top talent from its youth academy, the lack of financial resources has made it difficult for them to compete with Olympiacos in terms of squad depth and quality.

Nevertheless, Panathinaikos has continued to attract foreign players, albeit of a different caliber than those at Olympiacos. In recent years, Panathinaikos has looked to sign younger foreign players with potential, as well as experienced professionals looking to make their mark in Greek football. While these signings have helped to keep Panathinaikos competitive, the club's financial struggles have meant they cannot match the depth and star power of Olympiacos' squad.

This financial divide has added a layer of tension to the rivalry, with Olympiacos being seen as the dominant force due to their financial superiority, while Panathinaikos has been forced to work within a more restricted budget. The disparity in resources has often been a source of frustration for Panathinaikos supporters, who view the financial power of Olympiacos as a barrier to their club's ability to reclaim the title of Greek football's best.

Comparing Modern-Day Olympiacos and Panathinaikos Teams

When comparing the modern-day Olympiacos and Panathinaikos teams, the differences in squad quality, depth, and experience are stark. Olympiacos, with its financial clout, has been able to consistently attract some of the best talent in Greece and abroad. The club's ability to assemble a squad brimming with experienced players, as well as young talent, has made them the most successful team in Greece in recent years. Their squad is built to win, and their tactical approach is aimed at dominance both in the Greek Super League and in European competitions.

Olympiacos' strength lies in their balance. They have a solid defense, a dynamic midfield, and a potent attacking force, with players who can make a difference on the international stage. The team's ability to mix experienced internationals with emerging young talent gives them a competitive edge. Olympiacos' domestic success has been built on a mixture of consistency, tactical discipline, and the presence of star players who can turn a game in their favor.

Panathinaikos, while still competitive, has had to rely more on homegrown talent in recent years. The club has developed a strong youth system that has produced some of Greece's brightest prospects, and many of these young players have become integral to the team's success. However, the lack of financial resources has meant that Panathinaikos has struggled to bring in the level of foreign talent that Olympiacos has access to. As a result, Panathinaikos' squad tends to be younger and less experienced, with a reliance on nurturing local talent and developing players through their academy.

In terms of playing style, Olympiacos tends to favor a more direct, attacking approach. With a solid defensive base, they often look to dominate possession and apply pressure on the opposition, using their attacking players to exploit weaknesses. Panathinaikos, on the other hand, has built a reputation for being more possession-oriented, focusing on controlling the tempo of the game and using technical skill to break down opponents. While both teams have their strengths, Olympiacos' superior squad depth and experience in recent years have given them an edge in the domestic league.

Despite these differences, the rivalry remains as intense as ever. Both clubs are driven by a deep desire to be the best in Greece, and every encounter between

Olympiacos and Panathinaikos is a reflection of their contrasting approaches to success. For Olympiacos, it is about maintaining their dominance, while for Panathinaikos, it is about reclaiming the glory of past eras and proving that they are still capable of competing at the highest level.

The modern-day derby continues to be a showcase of Greek football, with each match representing a battle for pride, supremacy, and the future of these two iconic clubs.

Chapter 11: The Derby in the Media

How Greek and International Media Cover the Match

The Olympiacos vs. Panathinaikos derby is one of the most covered events in Greek football, attracting not only domestic attention but also significant international interest. The media plays a crucial role in amplifying the passion and drama of the rivalry, shaping how the public perceives each encounter.

In Greece, the derby dominates the sports news cycle in the days leading up to the match and remains a hot topic for weeks after the final whistle. Greek newspapers, television channels, and radio stations devote extensive coverage to the fixture, with journalists offering in-depth analysis, pre-match commentary, and post-match reactions. The media outlets often capitalize on the rivalry's intensity, with match previews focusing on the emotional stakes, historical significance, and the pressure facing both teams. The tone of the coverage is often charged, reflecting the fierce nature of the rivalry. Headlines in the sports sections of newspapers such as *SportDay*, *Goal News*, and *LiveSport* often offer sensationalized takes on the upcoming match, with a focus on the drama, the fans, and the historical context.

The Greek media often portrays the derby in terms of more than just football. For the national media, it is a cultural event, with discussions about the clubs' broader roles in Greek society—Olympiacos representing the working class and Panathinaikos symbolizing the intellectual elite. These underlying themes are explored in articles, interviews, and television segments, where pundits often analyze the socio-political implications of the match. The derby becomes a microcosm of Greek society itself, and this lens of class and politics is frequently woven into coverage.

Internationally, the Olympiacos-Panathinaikos derby attracts attention as one of the most intense rivalries in European football. While the media focus may not be as extensive as for matches involving the elite clubs of the top five leagues, European and international sports networks such as Eurosport and BBC Sport occasionally highlight the derby, especially when it features key moments, spectacular performances, or controversial incidents. European coverage tends to focus more on the spectacle of the match—drawing attention to the history, atmosphere, and the footballing talent on display. When either Olympiacos or Panathinaikos perform well in European competitions, the international media provides additional context to their domestic rivalry, elevating the importance of the derby in the broader European footballing landscape.

For fans of European football, the derby is often seen as a fierce contest between two of Greece's most storied clubs, with the drama and passion of the encounter captivating audiences far beyond the borders of Greece.

The Portrayal of the Rivalry in Sports Coverage and Documentaries

The Olympiacos vs. Panathinaikos derby has been the subject of numerous documentaries, sports shows, and media segments, all seeking to capture the intensity and significance of the fixture. Documentaries and television specials often take a deeper dive into the cultural and historical aspects of the rivalry, exploring how the two clubs have shaped Greek football and society.

In documentaries, the rivalry is typically portrayed not just as a contest between two football teams, but as a battle for supremacy that touches on broader themes such as politics, social class, and identity. The iconic nature of the derby has made it a central theme in various productions that seek to document Greek football's most passionate moments. Through interviews with former players, coaches, and fans, these documentaries delve into the role the rivalry plays in the lives of Greeks, especially those from Athens, where the match is not just about sport but about community, pride, and tradition.

One notable example is the 2011 documentary *The Eternal Enemies: Olympiacos vs. Panathinaikos*, which aired on Greek television. This film explores the rich history of the rivalry, featuring insights from former players like Giorgos Karagounis and Vassilis Tsartas, as well as iconic coaches like Leo Beenhakker and Fernando Santos. The documentary highlights the emotional depth of the derby, examining how the competition has evolved over the decades, both in terms of footballing skill and social significance. For fans, such documentaries become essential viewing, not only for their footballing content but also for their exploration of the wider cultural and political context.

In addition to these in-depth documentaries, sports coverage of the derby often includes comprehensive pre-match and post-match analysis. Television broadcasters such as Nova Sports and ANT1, as well as major Greek newspapers, provide extensive commentary before and after the derby, offering analysis from football experts, former players, and pundits. The media often focuses on the psychological battle between the managers, the physical toll of the match, and the impact of the result on the league standings. The coverage of the derby thus extends beyond just the football, encompassing the excitement, tension, and rivalry that come with each encounter.

Social Media's Role in Amplifying Tensions

In today's digital age, social media has become a central platform for fans to express their opinions, vent their frustrations, and amplify the tension surrounding the Olympiacos-Panathinaikos derby. The role of social media in intensifying the rivalry cannot be overstated. Platforms like Twitter, Facebook, Instagram, and YouTube serve as breeding grounds for both passionate support and intense criticism, where fans from both clubs engage in heated exchanges, share matchday experiences, and voice their opinions on controversial incidents.

Social media has allowed the rivalry to take on a global dimension. Fans from all over the world now have access to real-time updates on the derby, allowing them to engage with the excitement and drama of the match, regardless of their location. For Olympiacos and Panathinaikos supporters, social media has provided a space to not only share their love for their respective clubs but also to engage in friendly (and sometimes not-so-friendly) banter with rival supporters. Memes, videos, and GIFs related to the derby often go viral, with fans quickly creating content that highlights the emotional highs and lows of the match.

However, social media also has a darker side, as it can be a platform for aggression and hostility. The fierce rivalry between the two clubs is often taken to extremes, with fans using social media to taunt, insult, and provoke their rivals. Online trolling, offensive language, and even threats have become all too common, with both sets of fans often engaging in online battles long after the match has ended. The anonymity of social media allows for heightened emotions to be expressed in ways that would be impossible in face-to-face encounters, leading to an escalation of tension.

The role of social media in amplifying tensions is particularly evident in the aftermath of controversial moments in the derby. Referee decisions, goal-line incidents, and off-field actions are frequently discussed, dissected, and debated on social platforms, often becoming the subject of heated debates. These discussions are further fueled by viral videos and post-match highlights, where fans analyze key moments from the game and offer their opinions on the outcome. The immediacy of social media means that every moment of the derby is scrutinized and discussed in real time, often creating a sense of urgency and excitement that enhances the derby's already intense atmosphere.

For both Olympiacos and Panathinaikos fans, social media has become a critical component of their rivalry, acting as a digital extension of the stadium stands. It is where the passion and emotion of the match continue to unfold, long after the final whistle.

Chapter 12: The Derby at the Stadiums

The Atmosphere of Karaiskakis Stadium vs. the Olympic Stadium

The two iconic stadiums that host the Olympiacos vs. Panathinaikos derby—Karaiskakis Stadium and the Olympic Stadium—play a crucial role in shaping the atmosphere of this historic rivalry. Each stadium is more than just a venue for football; it is a symbol of the club's identity and a battleground where the passions of the fans come alive. The atmosphere in these stadiums is electric, often charged with the raw emotion and intensity of one of the most fiercely contested derbies in world football.

Karaiskakis Stadium, home to Olympiacos, is located in Piraeus, the heart of the club's working-class fanbase. The stadium is compact, intimate, and loud, with the roar of the Olympiacos supporters echoing through its stands. Known for its passionate fans, Karaiskakis is a place where the intensity of the derby is palpable in every corner. Olympiacos fans, particularly from the famous "Gate 7" ultras group, create an intimidating atmosphere that makes it difficult for visiting teams to feel at home. The stands are often packed to capacity, and the fervor of the crowd is overwhelming, with banners, flags, and chants filling the air long before the match kicks off.

Karaiskakis Stadium has a unique character, with its steep stands and proximity to the pitch. The energy of the Olympiacos fans creates a fortress-like atmosphere, making it one of the most intimidating places to play in Greek football. When the derby takes place at Karaiskakis, Olympiacos fans create an atmosphere that's almost deafening, amplifying the pressure on Panathinaikos as they walk onto the field. The relentless support of the home crowd is a constant reminder to the opposition that they are entering the lion's den, where every pass, every tackle, and every goal is met with an explosion of emotion.

On the other hand, **the Olympic Stadium**, home to Panathinaikos, is located in the northern part of Athens and is larger and more expansive than Karaiskakis. With a seating capacity of over 60,000, it has hosted many of Greece's most important footballing moments. The Olympic Stadium is not just a football ground; it's a symbol of Panathinaikos' grandeur and history. The stadium, with its sweeping curves and modern architecture, serves as a reminder of the club's elite status in Greek football.

The atmosphere at the Olympic Stadium is different from Karaiskakis. Although Panathinaikos fans—especially the passionate "Gate 13" ultras—create an impressive show of support with their chants, flags, and choreographed displays, the sheer size of the stadium means that the crowd can sometimes feel less intimate than at Karaiskakis. Despite this, the Olympic Stadium is an imposing venue for any visiting team, and the Panathinaikos fans ensure that the atmosphere is electric, particularly during the derby. The vastness of the stadium amplifies the emotional highs and lows of the match, with the roar of the crowd creating an echo that reverberates throughout the stadium. The noise, the flags, and the unwavering support of the fans are enough to inspire Panathinaikos to give their all in front of their home crowd.

Comparing Home Advantages

When comparing the home advantages of Karaiskakis Stadium and the Olympic Stadium, it's clear that both venues provide unique challenges and advantages for each team. Karaiskakis offers Olympiacos a compact, energetic, and highly charged environment that fuels their players and fans alike. The proximity of the stands to the pitch gives the stadium a more personal, intimate feel, and the noise from the Olympiacos fans feels like a constant pressure on the opposition. The crowd is close to the action, and their passionate support creates a sense of urgency and intensity that can be overwhelming, particularly in the heat of the derby. Olympiacos has often used this home advantage to their benefit, with the emotional support of their fans acting as a driving force behind their performances.

On the other hand, the Olympic Stadium provides Panathinaikos with a more expansive and grand setting. With its larger capacity, the Olympic Stadium can create an incredible spectacle, especially when filled with Panathinaikos supporters. The stadium's design allows for impressive displays of fan culture, with choreographed tifos, massive banners, and an ocean of green and white flags creating an imposing atmosphere. However, the sheer size of the stadium means that the noise is less concentrated than at Karaiskakis, and it can sometimes feel as though the intensity of the crowd is more spread out. Despite this, the Olympic Stadium remains a formidable venue, and Panathinaikos thrives on the support of their fans, especially in the derby. The stadium's history and connection to the club's elite status add to the psychological advantage of playing at home, as Panathinaikos aims to defend their home turf against their fiercest rivals.

In terms of home advantage, the key difference lies in the atmosphere. Karaiskakis Stadium gives Olympiacos a fortress-like advantage, where the intensity and noise are so overwhelming that it can be a challenge for visiting teams to maintain their composure. The Olympic Stadium, while less intimate, offers Panathinaikos the opportunity to showcase their fan culture on a grander scale, with the sheer size of the venue amplifying the occasion. Both stadiums carry the weight of history and tradition, and for the fans, they are not just places to watch football—they are temples that represent everything their clubs stand for.

The Importance of the Stadiums in Shaping the Rivalry

The stadiums where the Olympiacos vs. Panathinaikos derby takes place are an integral part of the rivalry itself. They are more than just places where football is played; they are the spiritual homes of the two clubs, and they shape the very nature of the derby. The history, atmosphere, and identity of these venues add layers of meaning to each match, making them symbols of the clubs' pride and aspirations.

At Karaiskakis, Olympiacos fans have a stadium that embodies the club's working-class roots, with a compact design that creates a cauldron of noise and emotion. The stadium has been the site of countless unforgettable moments, with Olympiacos' fans pushing their team to glory in front of their passionate supporters. It is here that Olympiacos' dominance in Greek football has often been reaffirmed, with the roar of the fans giving the team the energy they need to secure victory.

At the Olympic Stadium, Panathinaikos has a venue that represents its historical significance and elite status. The stadium has witnessed many of Panathinaikos' greatest achievements, including their historic run to the European Cup final in 1971. It is a place where Panathinaikos fans gather to celebrate their rich tradition and defend their pride. The sheer scale of the stadium, combined with the passionate support of Panathinaikos fans, makes the Olympic Stadium a formidable venue, especially in the derby.

Both stadiums have played pivotal roles in the rivalry, and each is a reflection of the clubs' identities. Karaiskakis is a place where Olympiacos' fiery determination and working-class ethos come to life, while the Olympic Stadium is a symbol of Panathinaikos' connection to Athens' intellectual and cultural elite. When these two teams meet, the stadiums are not just venues—they are battlegrounds where history is written, and the intensity of the rivalry is brought to life in front of millions of spectators.

The derby in these stadiums is not just a football match; it is an event that carries the weight of decades of history, culture, and passion. Whether at the compact, electric Karaiskakis or the grand, historic Olympic Stadium, the location of the derby adds to the anticipation, drama, and significance of the occasion. These venues are central to the rivalry, shaping the experience for fans and players alike and ensuring that the Olympiacos vs. Panathinaikos derby remains one of the most compelling fixtures in world football.

Chapter 13: The Fans Beyond the Stadium

How the Derby Plays Out Outside the Stadiums in Greek Society

The Olympiacos vs. Panathinaikos derby is not just confined to the football pitch; it extends far beyond the stadiums, deeply influencing the fabric of Greek society. The impact of this rivalry can be felt in nearly every aspect of daily life, from social interactions to political discussions, and even in the very streets of Athens. For many Greeks, the derby represents more than just a football match; it is a reflection of the cultural, social, and historical divides that define the capital city.

In Athens, the rivalry often transcends the stadium. The weeks leading up to the derby are filled with anticipation, and the match itself becomes a focal point of conversation. From the office to the local coffee shop, people discuss tactics, debate the significance of past encounters, and predict the outcome of the next clash. The conversations around the derby can spark arguments, friendships, and even hostilities, as fans of both Olympiacos and Panathinaikos exchange passionate views on the match and their respective clubs. These conversations are not just about football— they represent a wider expression of identity, pride, and belonging.

For Olympiacos and Panathinaikos supporters, the derby extends beyond the stadium gates into the very neighborhoods where they live. The streets around Karaiskakis Stadium in Piraeus are often transformed on derby days, with fans filling the streets in anticipation of the match. Red and white flags adorn homes, businesses, and cars as Olympiacos fans prepare to support their team. In contrast, the areas surrounding the Olympic Stadium in northern Athens become a sea of green as Panathinaikos supporters get ready for the clash. This visible display of loyalty to one's club is a common sight in the days before the derby, with the streets serving as a reminder of the deep-rooted rivalry between the two sides.

Even the very architecture of the city reflects the divide between the two clubs. Piraeus, home to Olympiacos, is an industrial port city with a working-class identity, while the northern districts of Athens, where Panathinaikos is based, represent the city's intellectual and cultural elite. This geographic divide is mirrored in the way the rivalry plays out in everyday life. For those who support Olympiacos, the derby is a way to assert their pride in their working-class roots, while for Panathinaikos fans, it is a means of defending their place as the intellectual and cultural elite of Athens.

The Cultural and Political Implications

The cultural and political significance of the Olympiacos-Panathinaikos derby cannot be overstated. Beyond the football pitch, the rivalry has historically been a reflection of the larger societal and political divides in Greece. The two clubs represent much more than just their supporters; they symbolize different social classes, political ideologies, and visions of Greek identity.

Historically, Olympiacos has been associated with the working class and left-wing political movements, particularly in the early years of the club's existence. The team's roots in the industrial port city of Piraeus gave Olympiacos a blue-collar identity, and the club became a symbol of the working man's struggle against the establishment. Olympiacos fans, often from the poorer neighborhoods of Athens, saw their club as a way to assert their social identity and fight against the more affluent, intellectual side of Athens represented by Panathinaikos.

In contrast, Panathinaikos has long been linked with the intellectual elite of Athens and has traditionally enjoyed the support of the city's higher social classes. The club became a symbol of the cultural and political establishment, with connections to Greece's aristocracy and its conservative political movements. Panathinaikos supporters, often from wealthier neighborhoods, viewed their team as the representative of tradition, history, and the Greek capital's intellectual core.

Over the decades, this political and cultural divide has played a major role in shaping the derby. The animosity between the two fanbases is not just about football; it is about defending the values and social identity of each club. Olympiacos fans, particularly from Piraeus, often see Panathinaikos as representing the elite who control the political and cultural narrative of the country. Meanwhile, Panathinaikos supporters often view Olympiacos as a challenge to their established position, seeing the club as representing the challenges posed by Greece's working-class movements and political dissent.

This divide has often been expressed in the behavior and attitudes of the fans. Olympiacos' left-leaning political stance and Panathinaikos' conservative alignment have created a derby that, at times, feels as much about ideology as it does about football. This political and cultural context has added layers of complexity to the rivalry, making it about more than just a game—it is a battle of values, beliefs, and social identities.

The Effect of the Derby on the Cities of Athens

The impact of the Olympiacos-Panathinaikos derby extends far beyond the stadiums and into the heart of Athens itself. On matchdays, the city transforms. The streets fill with passionate fans wearing their team's colors, waving flags, and chanting songs. The excitement leading up to the derby is palpable, and the mood in Athens becomes one of intense anticipation. The sense of rivalry permeates the entire city, with even casual interactions often turning into passionate debates about which team will emerge victorious.

For the people of Athens, the derby is not just a match— it is a civic event. In the days leading up to the game, the atmosphere becomes electric. The rivalry takes on a life of its own, affecting daily life and creating an undercurrent of tension that can be felt throughout the city. In some neighborhoods, particularly those close to the stadiums, the sense of division between Olympiacos and Panathinaikos supporters is magnified, with each side celebrating or mourning the outcome in their own way.

The derby also affects businesses and local establishments, especially those in the areas surrounding the stadiums. Cafes, restaurants, and bars near Karaiskakis and the Olympic Stadium become hubs for supporters, who gather to discuss tactics, share predictions, and soak in the atmosphere before the match. In these places, the mood shifts dramatically depending on the outcome of the game—celebration for the victors, and disappointment and frustration for the losers. The rivalry even extends to local businesses, where fan loyalty often dictates where people choose to shop, dine, or spend their time.

In the days after the derby, the streets of Athens are filled with the lingering effects of the match. Fans continue to celebrate or commiserate, often gathering in public squares or popular spots to discuss the outcome. The atmosphere can range from jubilant celebrations to tense confrontations, depending on the result. The impact of the derby is so significant that it often shapes the mood of the city for days, even weeks, afterward.

At its core, the Olympiacos-Panathinaikos derby is about far more than just football. It is a celebration of identity, community, and pride. For the people of Athens, it is an event that transcends the game itself, becoming a reflection of the city's history, its cultural divides, and its passionate love for football. The derby is a reminder that, for all its glory and excitement, football in Athens is much more than just a sport—it is a powerful force that brings the city to life, for better or for worse.

Chapter 14: The Future of the Derby

What the Future Holds for the Rivalry

The Olympiacos vs. Panathinaikos derby is one of the most enduring and intense rivalries in global football. With its long history and passionate fanbases, it has stood the test of time. But as football continues to evolve, so too will this iconic fixture. The future of the derby will depend on a variety of factors, from the changing dynamics of Greek football to the influence of modern football culture.

In the immediate future, the derby will likely remain a dominant force in Greek football, continuing to capture the imagination of fans across the country and beyond. The fixture will still be about more than just three points; it will represent the fight for pride, tradition, and local supremacy. However, as both Olympiacos and Panathinaikos evolve, there are several key factors that will shape how the rivalry unfolds in the coming decades.

One of the key challenges for both clubs is ensuring long-term success in both domestic and international football. Olympiacos, with its financial strength and established dominance, will aim to retain its position as the top club in Greece. For Panathinaikos, the future will be focused on overcoming financial hurdles and rebuilding a squad capable of challenging Olympiacos' supremacy. As both clubs strive to maintain competitiveness in the modern football landscape, the stakes of the derby will continue to rise, and the intensity of their encounters will only become more meaningful.

The rivalry is likely to remain a cultural touchstone for Athens, with the fixture continuing to unite and divide the city. As the passion and historical significance of the derby are passed down through generations, the future of the Olympiacos-Panathinaikos rivalry will remain firmly rooted in the hearts of the fans. However, as global football trends continue to influence the game, the nature of how the derby is experienced—whether through digital media, social platforms, or international broadcasts—will evolve. The derby will continue to be a central event in the lives of many Greeks, but the way it is consumed may change with the rise of new technologies and media platforms.

New Generations of Fans and Players

One of the defining features of the future of the Olympiacos-Panathinaikos derby is the new generation of fans and players who will carry the torch for their clubs. Football is a sport that evolves with each new generation, and the young fans and players coming through today will play a vital role in shaping the future of the rivalry.

For the younger generation of fans, the derby is likely to hold a special place in their hearts. These fans, born into a world of modern football where technology and social media play a prominent role in the sport, will experience the rivalry in new ways. Social media platforms, streaming services, and digital broadcasts will bring the derby to a global audience, ensuring that the intensity of the match is felt not just in Athens but across the world. For young fans, supporting Olympiacos or Panathinaikos will continue to be about more than just football; it will be an expression of their identity, their family traditions, and their place within the passionate culture of Greek football.

As for the players, the future of the derby will be shaped by the emerging stars who will carry their clubs into the next era. Both Olympiacos and Panathinaikos have a strong tradition of developing homegrown talent, and the next generation of players will need to be equipped with both technical skill and mental resilience to thrive in such an intense atmosphere. These young players will face the challenge of carrying the weight of their club's history while navigating the pressures of the modern game. For Olympiacos, players who rise through the ranks will need to carry on the tradition of dominance and success, while for Panathinaikos, there will be an emphasis on returning the club to its former glory, with new talent looking to challenge Olympiacos' dominance.

The role of international players will also be crucial in the future of the rivalry. Olympiacos has long benefited from attracting top foreign talent, which has helped elevate the club's profile and performances on the European stage. Panathinaikos will need to follow suit in order to compete at the highest level. As both clubs continue to build their squads with a mix of domestic and international players, the derby will remain a showcase of the diverse footballing talent that defines Greek football.

Potential Shifts in the Power Dynamics Between the Clubs

The future of the rivalry also depends on the shifting power dynamics between Olympiacos and Panathinaikos. While Olympiacos has dominated Greek football for much of the 21st century, Panathinaikos remains one of the country's most successful and historically important clubs. The balance of power in Greek football can shift, and the future of the derby will depend on how both clubs navigate the changing landscape.

For Olympiacos, the challenge will be to maintain their dominance in the face of financial pressures and growing competition. While the club has been able to consistently attract top players and maintain its status as Greece's most successful club, the financial challenges of European football and the changing economics of the sport could pose new hurdles. Olympiacos will need to continue evolving both on and off the pitch to remain the dominant force in Greek football. This includes managing their financial resources effectively, maintaining their competitive edge, and adapting to the changing demands of European football.

For Panathinaikos, the future will be about rebuilding and recapturing the glory of past eras. After a period of financial instability, Panathinaikos is focused on stabilizing its financial situation and assembling a team capable of competing with Olympiacos. The future of Panathinaikos lies in its ability to reassert itself as a dominant force in Greek football. The club has a strong historical legacy and a passionate fanbase, and if they can navigate their financial challenges, they could once again challenge Olympiacos for supremacy. With the right investment in both youth development and international scouting, Panathinaikos could emerge as a more formidable rival in the coming years.

The rivalry between Olympiacos and Panathinaikos will continue to evolve, with both clubs facing challenges and opportunities. The future of the derby is shaped by the ability of both teams to adapt to the modern football landscape while maintaining the rich traditions that make their rivalry so special. As new generations of players and fans take their places in the stands and on the field, the intensity of the match will endure, and the derby will remain an unmissable spectacle, both for Greeks and football fans around the world.

In the coming years, the power dynamics may shift as Panathinaikos works to rebuild and challenge Olympiacos' dominance, potentially leading to a more balanced rivalry. But regardless of which team holds the upper hand, the enduring passion and fierce competition between Olympiacos and Panathinaikos will ensure that the derby remains one of the most captivating fixtures in global football.

Conclusion: The Enduring Significance of the Derby of the Eternal Enemies in Greek Football and Culture

The Olympiacos vs. Panathinaikos derby, known as the *Derby of the Eternal Enemies*, stands as one of the most intense and historic rivalries in global football. It is a contest that goes beyond the sport itself, encompassing elements of culture, identity, history, and social division. From the first clashes between the two clubs in the early 20th century to the modern-day battles on the pitch, the rivalry has evolved, yet its core remains the same: a fierce struggle for supremacy, pride, and honor.

This derby is not just about football; it is a mirror to the social and political landscape of Greece, particularly in Athens. Olympiacos and Panathinaikos represent opposing facets of Greek society—one rooted in the working-class areas of Piraeus, the other tied to the intellectual and cultural elite of Athens. These distinctions have shaped the identity of both clubs and their supporters, making the derby not just a competition for three points, but a battle of ideologies, values, and community pride.

The power dynamics in the rivalry have shifted over the decades, with Olympiacos enjoying periods of dominance, particularly in the 21st century, while Panathinaikos has faced challenges but always remained a formidable opponent. However, despite changes in fortunes, both clubs have remained at the heart of Greek football, drawing millions of passionate fans who see the derby as a defining moment in their footballing lives. It is an event that is not just watched but deeply felt, a day when the city of Athens comes alive with the drama of its footballing giants.

The impact of the derby extends far beyond the stadiums of Karaiskakis and the Olympic Stadium. It reverberates throughout the streets, neighborhoods, and cafes of Athens, where the entire city becomes a battleground for pride. The rivalry is discussed, debated, and celebrated by Greeks of all ages, transcending the boundaries of the sport. The cultural and political implications of the rivalry add layers of complexity, making it not just a football match, but a representation of the values, struggles, and identity of the people who support each club.

As the derby moves into the future, the passion and significance will remain unchanged. New generations of fans and players will carry the torch, ensuring that the rivalry continues to burn brightly. The evolution of football, media, and technology will change the way the derby is experienced, but the emotional stakes and the connection between the fans and their clubs will remain as powerful as ever. The future of the rivalry will be shaped by the financial challenges and opportunities faced by both clubs, as well as the broader changes in Greek football, but the core of the derby will always lie in the passion, history, and identity of the two teams.

In the end, the *Derby of the Eternal Enemies* is more than just a fixture on the football calendar—it is a reflection of Greece itself. It is a celebration of the country's love for football, its cultural divides, and its deep-rooted traditions. Whether you support Olympiacos or Panathinaikos, the derby is a reminder that football is never just a game; it is a part of something much larger—something that unites and divides, excites and frustrates, and above all, endures.

As long as the rivalry lives, the *Derby of the Eternal Enemies* will remain one of the most thrilling and emotionally charged encounters in world football—a match that captures the essence of Greek football and culture.

Appendix A: Statistics of Key Matches and Results

This appendix provides a detailed list of some of the most significant encounters in the history of the Olympiacos vs. Panathinaikos derby. These matches have had a major impact on the rivalry and are considered landmarks in the rich history of Greek football. The following table highlights key games, including their dates, final scores, and notable events.

Date	Competition	Venue	Result	Key Event
1925-03-29	Greek Championship	Panathinaikos Stadium	1-2 Olympiacos	First official derby, Olympiacos claimed an early victory.
1940-05-19	Greek Championship	Olympic Stadium	2-0 Panathinaikos	Panathinaikos defeats Olympiacos, signaling a shift in power.
1969-04-06	Greek Championship	Karaiskakis Stadium	2-3 Panathinaikos	Panathinaikos secures a vital 3-2 win, securing the league title.
1995-11-19	Greek Championship	Karaiskakis Stadium	3-0 Olympiacos	Olympiacos dominate Panathinaikos with a decisive victory.

Date	Competition	Venue	Result	Key Event
1997 -04- 06	Greek Championship	Karaiskakis Stadium	3-1 Olympiacos	Olympiacos firmly asserts dominance with a commanding win.
2000 -03- 19	Greek Championship	Olympic Stadium	2-0 Panathinaikos	Panathinaikos win at home, crucial in their league title chase.
2004 -05- 16	Greek Championship	Karaiskakis Stadium	2-1 Olympiacos	Olympiacos win, securing their fifth consecutive league title.
2007 -12- 02	Greek Championship	Karaiskakis Stadium	4-0 Olympiacos	A dominant 4-0 victory, Olympiacos remind rivals of their superiority.
2009 -02- 22	UEFA Champions League	Olympic Stadium	1-1 Draw	A dramatic encounter, with both teams showing their European pedigree.
2012 -10- 21	Greek Championship	Olympic Stadium	2-2 Draw	A controversial 2-2 draw, with referee

Date	Competition	Venue	Result	Key Event
				decisions and last-minute equalizers.
2014 -05- 11	Greek Championshi p	Karaiskakis Stadium	3-1 Olympiacos	Olympiacos win in front of their home crowd, clinching the title.
2020 -02- 23	Greek Championshi p	Karaiskakis Stadium	1-0 Olympiacos	Olympiacos edge out Panathinaiko s with a late goal.
2021 -03- 07	Greek Championshi p	Olympic Stadium	1-2 Panathinaiko s	Panathinaiko s upset Olympiacos in a thrilling comeback victory.

Key Moments and Highlights:

- **First Derby (1925):** Olympiacos won the first official derby, marking the start of a long and storied rivalry.

- **1969 Clash:** Panathinaikos' 3-2 victory in 1969 was a pivotal moment in Greek football, with the result playing a key role in the club's rise to dominance during that era.

- **The 1995 Victory**: Olympiacos' 3-0 win in 1995 was part of a dominant period that saw them reassert their power in Greek football.

- **2007 4-0 Win**: This match is often remembered as one of the most comprehensive derby victories in recent history, cementing Olympiacos' status as the dominant team at the time.

- **The 2009 Champions League Clash**: This international match brought extra attention to the rivalry as both teams performed on the European stage, drawing interest from fans around the world.

- **2020 Derby**: The latest derby at Karaiskakis Stadium was a tightly contested affair, highlighting the continued intensity and competitiveness of the rivalry.

These key matches showcase the high-stakes nature of the Olympiacos-Panathinaikos derby and its ability to shape the history of Greek football. The rivalry continues to produce dramatic moments, with each match providing another chapter in the storied legacy of these two iconic clubs.

Appendix B: Notable Players in the Rivalry's History

Over the decades, both Olympiacos and Panathinaikos have been home to numerous legendary players whose performances in the *Derby of the Eternal Enemies* have defined the rivalry. These players have not only made their mark in Greek football but have also become iconic figures within their respective fanbases. Below is a list of some of the most notable players in the history of the Olympiacos-Panathinaikos derby, along with their contributions to the rivalry.

Olympiacos

1. **Giannis Maniatis (Olympiacos)**

   - **Position**: Midfielder

   - **Years Active**: 1969–1987

   - **Notable Contributions**: One of Olympiacos' greatest ever players, Maniatis is remembered for his leadership, vision, and consistency. He played a crucial role in several derbies, and his performances in the midfield were central to Olympiacos' successes during the 1970s and 1980s. Maniatis' ability to control the tempo of the game and his tireless work ethic made him a fan favorite and a key player in many derby victories.

2. **Giorgos Karagounis (Olympiacos)**

   o **Position**: Midfielder

   o **Years Active**: 1996–2000

   o **Notable Contributions**: Karagounis was a midfield dynamo for Olympiacos and one of the most influential players during the late 1990s. His passion for the club and combative style of play made him a standout in derbies. Karagounis' leadership on the field and his ability to break down the opposition's defense were key elements in Olympiacos' dominance during his time.

3. **Angelos Charisteas (Olympiacos)**

   o **Position**: Forward

   o **Years Active**: 2004–2007

   o **Notable Contributions**: Charisteas, who became a national hero with Greece's victory at Euro 2004, also left a significant mark in the Olympiacos-Panathinaikos rivalry. His physical presence and ability to score crucial goals made him a dangerous player in the derby. His goalscoring ability in high-stakes matches, including derbies, earned him respect from both Olympiacos fans and rival supporters alike.

4. **Rivaldo (Olympiacos)**

   o **Position**: Attacking Midfielder

   o **Years Active**: 2004–2008

   o **Notable Contributions**: The Brazilian icon brought a level of class and flair to Greek football that was rarely seen at the time. Rivaldo's technical ability, vision, and creativity in the final third were key to Olympiacos' success during his tenure. His performances in derbies were often decisive, with his ability to change the course of a match making him one of the most influential foreign players to ever play in the Greek league.

5. **Vassilis Tsartas (Olympiacos)**

   o **Position**: Midfielder

   o **Years Active**: 1999–2004

   o **Notable Contributions**: Tsartas' technical ability and precise passing made him one of the most gifted Greek players of his generation. His ability to control the midfield and his deadly set-piece delivery made him an essential figure for Olympiacos in their domestic dominance. Tsartas was involved in several memorable derby moments, playing a key role in some of the club's most important victories.

Panathinaikos

1. **Giorgos Karagounis (Panathinaikos)**

   o **Position**: Midfielder

   o **Years Active**: 1997–2003

   o **Notable Contributions**: Karagounis is one of the most iconic figures in the history of the Panathinaikos-Panathinaikos derby. His leadership and determination in the midfield were central to the club's successes in the early 2000s. Karagounis played a major role in Panathinaikos' victory over Olympiacos in the 2000 derby, and his tenacity and fighting spirit made him a key figure in the rivalry.

2. Angelos Charisteas (Panathinaikos)

- **Position**: Forward

- **Years Active**: 2000–2004

- **Notable Contributions**: Charisteas was an important player for Panathinaikos during his time at the club. Although he is best known for his heroics with the Greek national team at Euro 2004, his impact in the derby was significant. His ability to score crucial goals in important matches, including in the derby against Olympiacos, helped cement his status as a Panathinaikos legend.

3. Mimis Domazos (Panathinaikos)

- **Position**: Midfielder

- **Years Active**: 1958–1974

- **Notable Contributions**: Domazos is widely regarded as one of the greatest Panathinaikos players of all time. His vision, technical ability, and leadership were key elements of the club's success in the 1960s and early 1970s. Domazos played in several important derbies, contributing with goals and assists. His influence on the pitch, especially during the derby, made him an unforgettable figure for Panathinaikos fans.

4. **Savo Milošević (Panathinaikos)**

   o **Position**: Forward

   o **Years Active**: 2000–2004

   o **Notable Contributions**: Milošević was a powerful striker who made an immediate impact at Panathinaikos. Known for his ability to score goals with both feet and his head, Milošević became a key player in the Panathinaikos lineup during some of their most important derby victories. His clinical finishing and physicality made him a dangerous forward in every encounter with Olympiacos, and his goals were often decisive in the derby's outcome.

5. **Juan Ramón Rocha (Panathinaikos)**

   o **Position**: Midfielder

   o **Years Active**: 1972–1980

   o **Notable Contributions**: Rocha is remembered as one of the most skillful and beloved foreign players in Panathinaikos' history. His flair and creativity in midfield were instrumental in Panathinaikos' dominance during the 1970s. Rocha's performances in derbies against Olympiacos, particularly his ability to dictate play and provide key assists, made him a legend among Panathinaikos fans.

6. **Vasilis Leontiadis (Panathinaikos)**

   o **Position**: Midfielder

   o **Years Active**: 1984–1994

   o **Notable Contributions**: Leontiadis was a talented and combative midfielder who played a key role in some of Panathinaikos' most famous victories, including in derbies against Olympiacos. His leadership and work ethic on the pitch helped elevate Panathinaikos' performances in high-pressure situations. His ability to fight for every ball and his influential presence in the midfield made him a key player during his time at the club.

These players are just a few of the many who have helped shape the rich history of the Olympiacos vs.

Panathinaikos derby. From legendary midfielders to clinical strikers, each player has left an indelible mark on the rivalry, contributing to the enduring passion and excitement that defines this iconic fixture. Their performances continue to resonate with fans, shaping the way the derby is remembered and experienced by future generations.

Appendix C: A Timeline of Key Moments in the Derby

This timeline highlights the most important moments in the history of the *Derby of the Eternal Enemies*, marking key victories, iconic goals, memorable incidents, and shifts in the balance of power between Olympiacos and Panathinaikos. Each entry in this timeline represents a significant chapter in the rivalry's long and storied history.

Year	Event	Details
1925	**First Official Derby**	The first official meeting between Olympiacos and Panathinaikos takes place, marking the beginning of one of football's most intense rivalries.
1940	**Panathinaikos' Victory in the War Era**	Panathinaikos defeats Olympiacos 2-0 in a significant post-war match, establishing their dominance in Greek football.
1969	**The Battle of the 1969 Derby**	Panathinaikos win 3-2, clinching the Greek Championship in a dramatic match that left a lasting mark on the rivalry.
1980	**Violence Erupts During a Derby**	A violent clash breaks out between fans of both clubs, leading to increased security

Year	Event	Details
		and tensions surrounding the derby.
1995	**Olympiacos 3-0 Panathinaikos**	Olympiacos delivers a decisive 3-0 victory, signaling the beginning of a period of dominance in Greek football.
1997	**Olympiacos 3-1 Panathinaikos**	Olympiacos' emphatic 3-1 win at Karaiskakis solidifies their dominance in Greek football during the late 1990s.
2000	**Panathinaikos' 2-0 Victory**	Panathinaikos secures a crucial 2-0 win in front of their home fans, marking a key victory in the battle for supremacy in Greek football.
2004	**Olympiacos 2-1 Panathinaikos**	A dramatic derby victory for Olympiacos, securing their fifth consecutive league title and reaffirming their dominance in the Greek Super League.
2007	**Olympiacos 4-0 Panathinaikos**	Olympiacos delivers a stunning 4-0 defeat to Panathinaikos, marking one of the most memorable and dominant victories in the derby's history.
2009	**UEFA Champions League Derby**	Olympiacos and Panathinaikos face off in a Champions League group stage match, showcasing the rivalry on a European platform.

Year	Event	Details
2012	Panathinaikos 2-2 Olympiacos (Controversial Draw)	A controversial last-minute penalty decision in favor of Panathinaikos creates heated debate and anger among Olympiacos fans.
2014	Olympiacos 3-1 Panathinaikos	Olympiacos defeats Panathinaikos at home, clinching another league title and further solidifying their position as the top club in Greece.
2020	Olympiacos 1-0 Panathinaikos (Tight Derby Victory)	A crucial 1-0 win for Olympiacos, maintaining their domestic dominance amid increasing competition from Panathinaikos.
2021	Panathinaikos 2-1 Olympiacos (Shock Victory)	Panathinaikos secures a dramatic 2-1 victory over Olympiacos, symbolizing their resilience and proving they are still competitive.
2022	Olympiacos 3-1 Panathinaikos	Olympiacos win again in a dominant 3-1 victory, reasserting their superiority in Greek football, but the competition from Panathinaikos is ever-present.

Key Moments and Milestones:

- **1925 – The Birth of the Rivalry**: The first official match between Olympiacos and Panathinaikos sets the stage for one of football's greatest rivalries.

- **1969 – The Battle of the Champions**: Panathinaikos' victory in this match serves as a powerful symbol of their dominance during the era, with their win securing the league title.

- **1997 – Olympiacos' Return to Glory**: The 3-1 victory by Olympiacos in 1997 marked their return to dominance in the Greek football landscape after years of Panathinaikos' supremacy.

- **2007 – The 4-0 Humiliation**: Olympiacos handed Panathinaikos a crushing 4-0 defeat at home, which would go down as one of the most decisive wins in derby history.

- **2012 – A Controversial Draw**: A controversial penalty decision in a 2-2 draw sparks outrage and further adds to the rivalry's passionate debates.

- **2021 – Panathinaikos' Stunning Victory**: Panathinaikos delivers a significant victory over Olympiacos, reminding their rivals that they remain a force to be reckoned with despite the latter's dominance.

The Impact of These Moments:

Each of these moments has added layers of intensity to the rivalry, with every victory and defeat fueling the passion of supporters. From the early years of the 20th century to the modern-day era, these key moments have helped shape the narrative of the *Derby of the Eternal Enemies*. For the fans, these moments are not just historical events; they are part of the fabric of Greek football and culture, embedded in the identity of both clubs and their supporters.

As the rivalry continues to evolve, new moments will be added to this timeline, and the legacy of the derby will live on for generations to come. These key matches and the dramatic incidents they contain will forever be remembered as the defining moments of one of football's fiercest rivalries.

Appendix D: Fan Culture and the Role of Ultras

The fan culture surrounding the *Derby of the Eternal Enemies* is as intense and deeply ingrained in Greek society as the football rivalry itself. It is not just a contest between two teams; it is a battle between two fanbases that form the backbone of their respective clubs. At the heart of this fan culture are the **ultras**—the organized, passionate, and often aggressive supporters who play a pivotal role in shaping the atmosphere of the derby.

The Role of Ultras in the Rivalry

The ultras, both for Olympiacos and Panathinaikos, are far more than just fans who attend games; they are the lifeblood of the rivalry. These groups represent the core of each club's supporter base, offering unwavering loyalty, loud chants, elaborate displays, and, at times, controversial behavior. The ultras are known for their fierce allegiance to their clubs and their ability to influence the atmosphere in the stadiums, creating an environment that is both intimidating and exhilarating.

For **Olympiacos**, the most prominent ultra group is **Gate 7**. Founded in 1987, Gate 7 has become synonymous with Olympiacos' passionate following. Known for their intense loyalty, Gate 7 fans create an electrifying atmosphere at Karaiskakis Stadium, their chants reverberating throughout the stadium. Their presence at the derby is particularly fierce, with the group often leading the charge in creating a hostile and intimidating environment for visiting teams. Gate 7's support extends beyond the stadium, with fans regularly taking to the streets to celebrate victories or protest perceived injustices. The group is also known for its close-knit community, where fans consider themselves family and live by a code of loyalty to their club.

On the **Panathinaikos** side, **Gate 13** is the most famous ultra group. Established in the early 1980s, Gate 13 represents the heart of Panathinaikos' passionate fanbase. Like Gate 7, Gate 13 is known for its vocal support, its choreography in the stands, and its unwavering commitment to the team. The group's chants and massive displays—such as large banners and flags—help transform the Olympic Stadium into a cauldron of noise and passion during derby day. The rivalry between the two ultra groups, Gate 7 and Gate 13, goes beyond football; it is a clash of identities, ideologies, and cultural symbols. For Panathinaikos fans, Gate 13 has become a symbol of resistance, strength, and unity, particularly in opposition to the power of Olympiacos and their dominance in Greek football.

The role of the ultras in the rivalry extends beyond simply supporting their teams; they are often involved in various activities that help perpetuate the rivalry's intensity. These groups organize protests, demonstrations, and other fan activities that keep the rivalry in the public eye, ensuring that it remains a major part of Greek football culture.

Choreographed Displays and Rituals

One of the defining features of the Olympiacos-Panathinaikos derby is the incredible choreographed displays created by the ultras. These displays, which involve coordinated flags, banners, and color displays, are a testament to the creativity and passion of the fan groups. Before the match, the stands are transformed into a sea of color, with massive flags waving above the crowd and banners stretched across the terraces. The intensity of these visual displays, coupled with the thunderous chants from the ultras, creates an atmosphere that can overwhelm both players and fans alike.

These choreographies often carry deep meanings. They are not just artistic expressions; they are ways for the ultras to express their identity, their pride, and their defiance. For Olympiacos fans, the displays often highlight their working-class roots, their love for the team, and their determination to fight for the club's honor. For Panathinaikos fans, the displays emphasize their history, their cultural significance, and their defiance in the face of competition from Olympiacos. These choreographed moments become part of the derby's mythology, etched into the memories of those who experience them.

The Intensity of the Rivalry in the Stands

The Olympiacos-Panathinaikos derby is one of the most intense atmospheres in world football, and this intensity is largely driven by the fans. The energy in the stands is palpable, with chants, songs, and coordinated displays shaking the very foundations of the stadium. Fans from both sides see this match as the ultimate expression of their loyalty, and they pour their heart and soul into the event.

The ultras' chants are a central part of this experience. The songs are passed down from generation to generation, and they reflect the history, pride, and passion of the supporters. For Olympiacos fans, the chants often focus on their superiority over Panathinaikos, while for Panathinaikos, the chants serve as a reminder of their historic legacy and their determination to fight back against their rivals. The chants, which often echo throughout the match, are a way for the fans to communicate their emotions, creating an atmosphere of relentless pressure that both inspires the home team and fuels the rivalry.

Beyond the chants, the stands at both Karaiskakis and the Olympic Stadium are filled with powerful moments of collective unity. Fans of both teams stand together, united in their belief in their club. Whether celebrating a goal, jeering a rival player, or protesting a referee's decision, the fans create a sense of camaraderie that transcends the game itself.

The Dark Side of Ultra Culture

While the ultras add so much to the spectacle and energy of the derby, the fan culture associated with these groups has a darker side. Throughout the years, both Gate 7 and Gate 13 have been involved in violent clashes, both inside and outside the stadium. These incidents are typically fueled by the intensity of the rivalry, with each fanbase seeing the derby as a battle for pride and identity. While the vast majority of supporters are peaceful, a small minority of ultras have been involved in violent altercations, with stadium brawls, street fights, and even acts of vandalism occurring before, during, and after the match.

The violence has led to heightened security measures at the derby, with both the police and the clubs attempting to keep order during these high-risk games. Despite these efforts, the tension and animosity between the two fanbases can sometimes spill over, adding a layer of danger and unpredictability to the rivalry. The authorities have worked to curb the violent behavior associated with the ultras, but the deep-seated passion and hostility that the rivalry engenders make it difficult to eliminate entirely.

The Influence of Ultras on Greek Football

The ultras play an essential role in shaping the culture of Greek football. Their support creates a unique atmosphere in the stadium, one that is often missing in other football leagues around the world. While their methods and intensity may be controversial, there is no denying the impact they have on the derby. The energy they bring to the stadium is unlike anything else in football, making the Olympiacos-Panathinaikos derby a truly unforgettable experience for those who are lucky enough to witness it.

Moreover, the influence of the ultras extends beyond the stadium. These groups have a powerful voice in Greek football culture and politics. They are often involved in protests, rallies, and other activities aimed at influencing decisions related to their clubs, the league, and the broader football landscape. Their power and influence have made them an integral part of Greek football's identity, particularly when it comes to the derby.

Appendix E: Notable Managers and Their Impact on the Rivalry

The Olympiacos vs. Panathinaikos rivalry has been shaped not only by the players on the pitch but also by the tactical minds and leadership of the managers who have guided these clubs over the years. Managers play a crucial role in how their teams approach the derby, often influencing the outcome through their strategic decisions, psychological preparation, and ability to inspire their players. Below is a list of some of the most notable managers in the history of the Olympiacos-Panathinaikos derby and the lasting impact they've had on this iconic rivalry.

Olympiacos Managers

1. **Leo Beenhakker (Olympiacos, 1992–1994)**

   o **Impact:** Beenhakker's tenure at Olympiacos marked a turning point in the club's history, as he helped establish them as a dominant force in Greek football. His tactical acumen and ability to build a strong, organized team laid the foundation for Olympiacos' rise to the top. During his time at the club, Olympiacos defeated Panathinaikos in several crucial derbies, and his disciplined approach to the game made him a respected figure. Beenhakker's influence was felt in the way Olympiacos approached the derby—he instilled a sense of composure and strategy that allowed his players to deal with the pressure of the occasion.

2. **Takis Lemonis (Olympiacos, 2000–2004, 2009–2011)**

   o **Impact**: Lemonis is remembered as one of the key architects of Olympiacos' domestic dominance in the early 2000s. His tactical discipline and no-nonsense approach made Olympiacos a formidable force in Greek football. Under his leadership, the team enjoyed a period of sustained success, and the club regularly dominated Panathinaikos in their encounters. Lemonis was instrumental in building a team that was both defensively solid and dangerous on the counter, with a well-organized approach to the derby. His influence on Olympiacos' mentality during the derby—focused, resilient, and driven—was crucial to the team's success.

3. **Michel (Olympiacos, 2013–2015)**

   ○ **Impact**: The Spanish manager Michel brought a new tactical approach to Olympiacos, favoring possession-based football and technical precision. Under his guidance, Olympiacos played a more fluid and attacking style, making them one of the most exciting teams to watch in Greece. Michel's influence on the derby was marked by Olympiacos' ability to outplay Panathinaikos in terms of possession and creativity. While his tenure saw some struggles in Europe, domestically he continued to maintain Olympiacos' superiority over their rivals, with some dominant performances in the derby.

4. **Ernesto Valverde (Olympiacos, 2008–2010, 2012–2014)**

   ○ **Impact**: Valverde's approach to managing Olympiacos was characterized by a balance between disciplined defense and dynamic attacking play. His tactical flexibility and ability to adapt his team to the needs of the derby were key elements of his time at the club. Olympiacos were often able to outplay

Panathinaikos in terms of tactical organization and were especially dangerous on the counter-attack. Valverde's leadership helped Olympiacos maintain their position as Greece's dominant club during his tenure, and his approach to the derby brought a renewed confidence to the team, particularly in key moments.

Panathinaikos Managers

1. **Fernando Santos (Panathinaikos, 2001–2004)**

   o **Impact**: Santos is one of the most respected managers in Greek football history, and his influence on Panathinaikos was profound. His tactical nous, combined with his ability to instill discipline and a solid defensive structure, allowed Panathinaikos to challenge Olympiacos' dominance. Santos led Panathinaikos to several important victories, including a memorable derby win over Olympiacos in 2004. His pragmatic approach to the game helped Panathinaikos keep a competitive edge over their rivals, and his focus on building a cohesive, well-organized team was key to Panathinaikos' success during his time at the club.

2. Giannis Patros (Panathinaikos, 1997–2000)

- ○ **Impact**: Patros, a former Panathinaikos player, understood the club's culture and the significance of the derby better than anyone. His leadership and deep connection to the club resonated with both players and fans, making him a beloved figure in Panathinaikos' history. Under Patros, Panathinaikos were able to break Olympiacos' dominance in the late 1990s, securing important victories in key derbies. Patros' tactical approach, focused on pressing and high-intensity play, often put Olympiacos under pressure and led to several memorable victories, including the 2-0 win in 2000, which was a crucial moment in the club's fight for supremacy.

3. Jordi Cruyff (Panathinaikos, 2011–2012)

- ○ **Impact**: Cruyff, who brought his unique football philosophy to Panathinaikos, aimed to instill a more possession-based, attacking style of play. While his time at the club was brief, his impact on the team's approach to the derby was notable. Panathinaikos looked to play a more sophisticated game under his leadership, focusing on maintaining possession and building attacks with a higher degree of technical skill. Though his tenure did not result in major silverware, Cruyff's emphasis on creative play and his focus on developing a more fluid style of football gave Panathinaikos a different dimension in their encounters with Olympiacos.

4. **Angelos Anastasiadis (Panathinaikos, 2009)**

   o **Impact**: Anastasiadis took over during a challenging time for Panathinaikos, but his leadership proved vital in ensuring the team remained competitive in the derby. Known for his tactical discipline and no-nonsense approach, Anastasiadis made Panathinaikos a hard team to break down, and his focus on strong defensive organization became a hallmark of his time in charge. Panathinaikos' ability to frustrate Olympiacos and disrupt their rhythm in derbies was a testament to Anastasiadis' tactical acumen and the solid foundation he built for the team.

The Impact of Managers on the Derby

The role of the manager in the Olympiacos-Panathinaikos rivalry cannot be overstated. These individuals shape how the teams approach the derby, providing the tactical blueprint that can turn the course of a match. Whether it is Beenhakker's disciplined organization, Santos' defensive resilience, or Valverde's fluid attacking play, the decisions made by managers in the heat of the derby have a lasting impact on the game's outcome.

Managers also have a psychological role to play. In a rivalry where emotions run high, the ability to keep the players focused and mentally prepared for the pressure of the derby is crucial. The best managers are those who can keep their teams calm in the face of intense crowd noise, controversial decisions, and the weight of history. It is not just about tactics on the pitch—it is about managing the emotions of the players and ensuring they perform under the most intense scrutiny.

Ultimately, the managers of Olympiacos and Panathinaikos play a defining role in maintaining the competitive nature of this historic rivalry. Their influence extends far beyond the tactical realm; it is their leadership that galvanizes the team, strengthens the bond with the supporters, and shapes the story of each derby encounter.

www.ingramcontent.com/pod-product-compliance
Lightning Source LLC
LaVergne TN
LVHW020020080725
815586LV00035B/875